T0265762

"Enid's appreciation and skill with aroids is well-known and loved in the plant community. I was specifically excited to hear her stories and insights, which came through in her Collector's Notes for each plant featured in this book. This is a must-read for every aspiring aroid collector!"

—**Darryl Cheng**, creator of House Plant Journal
    and author of *The New Plant Parent*

"There's nothing more to say about Enid besides 'look at her damn plants.' Her generosity, attentiveness, and love for the plants she grows is evident in every leaf, stem, and root. She's not blessed to have this book, this book is blessed to have her, and so are we."

—**Tyler Thrasher**, artist/scientist/author

"With *Welcome to the Jungle*, Enid Offolter has given us all the inspiration we need to grow the best and rarest. This celebrated expert has created a must-read for anyone fascinated by the otherworldly beauty of tropical aroids, and experts and beginners alike will find a treasure trove of gorgeous photos and invaluable information among its pages."

—**Craig Miller-Randle**, TV presenter and author of *Green Thumb*

Welcome to the Jungle

ENID OFFOLTER

Welcome to the Jungle

Rare Tropical Houseplants to
Collect, Grow, and Love

PHOTOGRAPHS BY SONYA REVELL

TEN SPEED PRESS
California | New York

CONTENTS

Why Do We Love Plants?

Many of us are living in unnatural environments that are far removed from nature, in crowded apartment complexes on congested streets with bustling sidewalks. Studies have shown that nature deprivation is a prime cause of depression and anxiety; the more we are distanced from nature, the more anxiety we feel. It's no wonder that filling our homes with plants brings us peace and inspires us. Plants bring us joy and create calm. Walk into a green space, pause, close your eyes, take a deep breath, and pay attention to how you feel. Plants add so much life to a space, and they oxygenate and refresh the air we breathe. Taking care of plants gives us a way to nurture living things. It's just human nature to feel a sense of pride as each new leaf unfurls and it's wonderful to know that these beautiful, green beings depend on us for their care. Another amazing part of growing houseplants is the connection we share with an incredible community of fellow plant lovers. So many friendships are forged around common plant interests. I've met some of my best friends through our shared interest in plants.

In the two decades I've been collecting, I have amassed quite a few plants. It's my life. Like many other plant enthusiasts, my collection grew to a sizable number of common houseplants, such as fiddle-leaf fig (*Ficus lyrata*) and Swiss cheese plant (*Monstera deliciosa*), which thrived without any special care. These and many other popular houseplants are mass produced and easy to acquire and maintain. But eventually I was ready to kick it up a notch and add some extraordinary plants to my collection. If you're ready to add diversity to your plant collection, you'll find plenty of suggestions in this book on how to find and care for extraordinary plants, many of which are so beautiful they almost defy description.

CHAPTER ONE

Graduating from Common to Extraordinary Houseplants

I have always been interested in plants, nature, and anything unusual or different. Anytime I moved into a new house or apartment, the first thing on my to-do list would be to visit the local nursery and buy as many young plants and bags of topsoil as I could afford to make a garden in front of my new home. Before unpacking and before painting, I would plant a garden. I find it incredibly welcoming to come home and be surrounded by plants. To me, plants are the most important part of making a house a home.

In 1999, I discovered that I could buy plants on eBay. (Who knew, right?) As I became addicted to the thrill of winning plants at auction, it became apparent that I needed a way to fund my new plant addiction. So I started an online business from my Florida home, selling seeds on eBay—seeds that I would purchase in bulk and sell in smaller lots, or seeds that I collected from my own garden. When other sellers started offering seeds on eBay, I took it as a sign of my success. Imitation is the sincerest form of flattery, I suppose.

Eventually, to make more money to support my plant collecting habit and to increase my own collection, I began visiting nurseries and buying pots full of easy-to-grow plants, which I would divide and sell online. After a successful day of buying, I'd return home with a carload of plants, and then the real work would begin. I would divide the plants into several smaller clumps and repot the divisions, placing them on a makeshift plant bench to get them established. Some of these repotted plants would be sold online, and some I would keep for myself. This quickly spiraled out of control, however, and soon I had thousands of plants to care for—or maybe even hundreds of thousands!

When I started selling plants on the internet, most of the nursery owners I knew didn't take online plant sales seriously. In fact, I was actually embarrassed to admit that I sold plants on eBay. At that time, most of the nursery owners I knew were dismissive of my online nursery and plant shipping business. Today, however, some of those same people call me for advice on identifying plants and help with selling them online!

More and More Plants

After a while, I figured out how to build my own website, NSE Tropicals. Selling rare and unusual plants online was pretty easy, and there still wasn't a lot of competition at the time. Nevertheless, most buyers preferred to order from printed catalogs or chose to visit brick-and-mortar nursery locations, and some didn't believe this was a legitimate business because online plant sales were so new. So I began attending plant shows, providing landscaping services, and eventually opened a retail nursery. I did whatever it took to get by. Despite buying tons of advertising, my retail nursery location wasn't producing enough income to make a decent living. There simply wasn't enough local interest in rare plants, and I realized that the internet was the only way to reach buyers from across the United States. After three hurricanes in one year, and then the birth of my son (so make that four hurricanes), I realized that maintaining the nursery was actually more of a hindrance than a help. So after some thought, I went back to strictly online. That was the best decision ever. I often think it's crazy how hard I tried to get people to visit the nursery back then, while now I have to fight to keep them out because of the national popularity of NSE Tropicals.

Today, at NSE Tropicals, I propagate most of my new plants from my own collection. My Florida operation includes a greenhouse and three shade houses (structures that provide some shade but, unlike the greenhouse, are open to outside air circulation). Most of the plants grow best in either the greenhouse or in the wall shade house because the bright summer light in the other two shade houses can stress the plants. In the wall shade house is my first—and best—living wall (a vertical plant installation mounted on the wall), where water runs down

the wall of plants and breezes blow across it, making the shade house much cooler than the other two. My plants find it way more pleasant and they like it best—at least that's what they told me. I work in this shade house most of the time, and it also seems to be a favorite hangout for a diversity of life besides plants. With so many leafy places to hide and so much available water, it is home to many species of lizards, frogs, and the occasional snake. These guys help me out by devouring any pests they find.

The Jump to Aroids

There is no greater excitement than finding and growing new plants. As my plant collection has grown, my search for new additions has driven me to find more and more unusual and rare plants. When I visit a nursery, it seems I am constantly drawn to plants that aren't for sale. (Often, the more interesting and rare the plant, the less likely it will be for sale, because the nursery owner appreciates the plant too much to send it off to another home.) Because I've always been interested in the more unusual plants that the world has to offer, when I discovered aroids, I was hooked.

Aroids are a common name for the Araceae, or arum, family of tropical plants, known for their spectacular and leathery foliage, crazy inflorescences (flower clusters), and weird growth habits, which make them irresistible. Some aroids, such as the spiny *Lasia spinosa*, have spiraling inflorescences that resemble unicorn horns. Others, such as *Helicodiceros muscivorus*, are pollinated by flies. (Its common names are pig butt arum and dead horse arum, and there's a reason for this: its bloom looks and smells like the back end of an animal—complete with the tail!)

When I attended my first International Aroid Society (IAS) show at Fairchild Tropical Botanic Garden in Coral Gables, just outside Miami, I met many like-minded plant freaks and learned so much. With such a great plant community centered on aroids, the collectors, botanists, and explorers I met proved to be a priceless experience. Plants attract their own distinct groups of enthusiasts—for me, "aroiders" are the perfect fit, being equal part plant nerds and introverts.

PHILODENDRONS, MONSTERAS, AND ANTHURIUMS

The three best-known representatives of the aroid family are species of *Philodendron*, *Monstera*, and *Anthurium*, and these aroids are featured in this book.

Some philodendrons have incredibly showy leaves, velvet surfaces, fuzzy petioles (leaf stems), and variegation (leaf color variation) that add interest and texture. There's a philodendron to match each person's style, and their accommodating nature and ease of growth make them popular houseplants. Most philodendrons can handle less humidity (60 to 70 percent) than anthuriums, making them a bit better suited to indoor culture.

Monsteras are the undisputed king of the houseplants and acclimate well to indoor life. Like philodendrons, they require average humidity (60 to 70 percent) and most have dramatic tropical foliage, with naturally occurring fenestrations (holes and splits) in the leaves. There are many theories as to why the leaves have evolved in this way: perhaps the fenestrations enable light to reach the lower leaves of the plant as it climbs, or they may reduce wind resistance, or perhaps they fool insects into thinking that another insect has already taken up residence on the plant and chewed its leaves.

Anthuriums are among the best plants for indoor air purifying according to the 1989 NASA Clean Air Study, but they can be a bit of a challenge to grow indoors. They grow slower than either philodendrons or monsteras, they require more humidity (70 to 80 percent), and they are more sensitive to overwatering. Of the three genera, *Anthurium* seems to show the most species diversity, exhibiting a variety of shapes and sizes and fascinating foliage. Although there are two main types of anthuriums—those grown for their showy blooms (inflorescences) and those grown for their foliage—this book focuses on the foliage types.

Plant Failures and Successes

I could write a whole book on the plants I've killed . . . er, I mean loved to death. I can't stand looking at a plant with even a single half-brown leaf; it makes me sad, and I feel bad for any plant that suffers in my care. I am solely responsible for its health and welfare, and I agonize over possible solutions when a particular fussy plant takes a turn for the worse.

I have tried numerous times to grow *Anthurium cutucuense*, for example, but they continue to elude me. They may thrive for a little while in winter, but as soon as the weather heats up and I start to gloat about my mad plant-growing skillz, they self-destruct in defiance. I keep trying, after assuring myself that these plants probably weren't properly established when I bought them, or maybe they suffered during shipping. This *Anthurium* species might be one of those plants that decide to grow happily *under* the bench in the gravel after falling through the slats. (Maybe I should try that next. After all, there's a whole ecosystem thriving under my plant benches in the shade house, without any help from me.)

Another plant I had trouble growing in the beginning was *A. warocqueanum*. I'd heard such horrible stories about trying to keep this plant alive that I may have doomed it from the start. I was so sure it would be difficult, that perhaps I willed it to be so. Because it's hot in Miami for nearly twelve months of the year, and "warocqs" are known to be heat-hating prima donnas, I had resigned myself to never being able to grow one properly. But after I started growing them in the wall shade house, my success rate shot up. The living wall drips water into a catchment pond, and mist comes on every ten minutes for a few seconds, cooling the air substantially. Just in the past year, I set seed on *A. warocqueanum* twice in the wall shade house and grew thousands of little velvety baby plants.

One day as I surveyed my warocq kingdom, I realized that I'd learned something new with each failure. When a plant dies, I usually examine the situation like a forensic scientist: well, the soil is sopping wet, and it looks like the plant rotted. Or, wow, this poor plant is dry as a bone. There must have been a leaf blocking the sprinkler head. Interestingly, I have determined that the plants I set up correctly in the beginning and then leave alone do far better than some others I am trying to "care" for. I can't tell you how many times I have dumped the seemingly plantless soil from a pot out in the yard, only to have something wonderful pop up the following year in the same place with no help from me at all. Invariably, if I dig it up and put it in a pot with proper potting soil and fertilizer, and then pet it, love it, and name it George, it will wilt and die.

Learning from Nature

I've learned that if I'm having trouble with a particular plant, it can help to find out where and how it grows in nature. Realistically, it would be difficult to re-create a rainforest in your living room, but that shouldn't stop you from trying. Sometimes, I forget that plants in the same genus can require quite different growing conditions. For example, *A. clarinervium* is found in Chiapas, Mexico, where it grows as an epiphyte (a plant that uses its roots to attach itself to another plant, such as a tree, and draws moisture and nutrients from the surrounding environment). This species is accustomed to drier conditions than many other anthuriums. Its extra fleshy roots absorb moisture, and it seems to prefer brighter light than others in the same genus.

When you see the word *epiphyte* associated with a plant, you should treat that information as a clue that you'll need to pot it up in a very well-draining soil mix with lots of amendments such as orchid bark, perlite, and horticultural charcoal. If a wild plant grows attached to a tree in nature, you can bet that it doesn't want to sit in some soggy soil on a dark living room bookshelf. Most pendulous species of anthurium are epiphytes—growing on a tree gives them room to hang down. Think about it: Would you expect to see *A. pendulifolium* growing in the wild with its 6-foot long, pendulous leaves lying in the dirt? I'll answer that. No. You wouldn't.

Consider, for example, an interesting adaptation of a bird's nest anthurium: the whole plant grows in a funnel shape that channels rainwater to the roots, where it's needed most. You might imagine that many of these plants grow wild in areas of low rainfall, which they do, but they have high water needs, and the funnel shape helps them catch all the water they can when it rains. If you're growing a bird's nest anthurium such as *A. superbum* or *A. reflexinervium*, try dripping some water on one of the leaves and watch to see the water flow right to the roots. At the opposite end of the spectrum, many of the heart-shaped, velvety plant leaves have a built-in "drip tip" that helps them move excess water away from their leaves in the rainy season. This protects them from soggy roots that can later cause problems. The leaves' velvety texture also helps the plant channel and shed excess water.

The Demand for Aroids

In 2017, aroids became all the rage for plant collectors. Many of us who are in love with the beauty of aroids aren't surprised by this interest in an amazing genus. After all, an aroid can thrive indoors, and the plants have that coveted tropical look that styles well on social media. And yet, the sudden surge was unexpected. That year, I'd started writing a weekly newsletter, and I thought that perhaps the newsletter had something to do with the increased orders I was receiving. But when I started using Instagram, I realized this platform was the cause of the aroid frenzy, and the frenzy for houseplants in general.

As a collector who mostly propagates from existing plants in my shade houses, I was ill prepared for the onslaught of aroid plant requests, and I could not grow enough plants to meet the insatiable demand. Within weeks, tens of thousands of people were on waiting lists for plants, particularly the Pink Princess philodendron and variegated monstera. At the time, I probably had only three plants of each in my collection. As the collector craze spiraled toward other aroids, many of the exotic plants that I rarely sold became the subject of thousands of hopeful emails. Before this time, I felt fortunate even to be able to grow these kinds of plants, and I believed it was nothing short of a miracle that some of them were in cultivation at all.

At the beginning of 2020, I thought for sure that the COVID-19 pandemic would mark the end of the aroid craze. I mean, who buys plants when they've just lost their job and the world is in turmoil? Answer: everyone. As I was preparing for a slump, what actually happened was quite the opposite. As people spent more time at home, they realized that they had more time to care for plants! Being stuck at home helped many people realize that they could surround themselves with plant life, a positive addition to their home that could make them happy and help them get through tough times.

There was also a huge rise in the number of people who were propagating and selling plants online as a side hustle to make ends meet and to keep themselves busy. When you're in lockdown, the excitement of waiting for something beautiful and hopefully life changing in the mail is real. I kept thinking that this new craze would eventually slow down, but now I know better. As long as we live and work in apartments in crowded cities, creating tranquil green spaces in our homes will never go out of style.

The Future of the Exotic Plant Industry

It's hard to say what the future will bring. I keep expecting exotic plant sales to settle down. I mean, the interest in these amazing plants has escalated, but I tell myself that this can't be the new normal! But then it escalates even more.

With the public's increased interest in exotic plants, some growers are turning to tissue culture, aka micropropagation, to increase production of some formerly super rare plants. Producing and growing thousands of clones of a plant in a sterile nutrient solution such as agar offers many advantages to growers and collectors alike. First, plants can be propagated quickly. It may take years for a plant to produce seeds naturally, if it happens at all. But with tissue culture, hundreds of thousands of identical plants can be produced quickly. And these clones are produced free of pathogens, pests, and diseases.

There is a downside to cloned plants, however. If you plant anthurium seeds, for example, every seedling will be different; each will have variations in terms of vigor, leaf veining, leaf and flower color, and other aspects that you can't get with tissue-cultured plants. Because each cloned plant is genetically identical to the original parent plant, the clones can lose much of the interesting variation provided by seed-grown plants, and this can take some of the thrill and excitement out of collecting: After all, if everyone has access to thousands of identical plants that were once rare, the plants are no longer special. So what's the point of collecting them?

In addition, the best representation of a species is not always used in tissue culture. It's far more likely that the lab was given a plant to clone with little regard for whether it was an especially exceptional form. The availability of more tissue-cultured plants may lower their prices, but I think there will always be a few rare plants that continue to be in great demand and will therefore cost more.

I could probably make a living for the rest of my life by propagating the plants I already have, but of course a big part of the fun is finding and growing new plants. Many of the more interesting plants at local nurseries have been picked clean because of high demand, but there are still plenty of wonderful species to be found at plant shows and by trading with other plant collectors.

ETHICAL PLANT COLLECTION

It is exciting to see a new generation of plant people who are excited about growing plants. If people continue to propagate plants ethically, it will bring more balance to the industry—and more plants! Happily, more and more growers and collectors are involved in trying to propagate plants sustainably rather than collecting seeds or plants from their natural habitat.

When the plant craze first began, many people started poaching plants, or illegally removing plants from the wild, which sometimes cleared out whole populations of plants at one time. Some species have such a narrow natural range that a single overzealous collector can decimate an entire population. Some of these poached plants are very difficult to grow outside of their natural habitat or in greenhouse conditions, and they will never thrive after they arrive in people's homes.

A few years ago, as I was driving through Ecuador, I noticed a particular anthurium species growing beside the road. I wanted to find a good spot to pull over to snap a picture, but by the time we had driven another hundred feet to park, we were next to a completely different species. That's how small a habitat range can be. You can imagine how much damage someone could do to a particular population if they decided to collect all of it. If the plant occurs only in a small area and it's removed, it may be gone forever.

Mudslides were quite common when I was in Ecuador, and I thought it was interesting that plants that had been growing at the top of a range could suddenly be growing at the bottom in a matter of moments. (Botanist: "This plant grows at an altitude of 5,000 meters. . . . Oops! Make that 5 meters.") It seems that a single mudslide could destroy a whole population of a plant with a narrow natural range. But humans can do equal or even more widespread damage by collecting plants illegally, which is why it's important never to buy plants that have been poached (you'll read more about this in chapter two).

Plant Perfectionism

While visiting Ecuador, I made an interesting observation: Plants in situ have holes in their leaves. Lots of them. Leafcutter ants cut out sections of leaves using their powerful mandibles and take them back to their nests, where they use them to grow a type of fungus that they eat. The ants don't mess around, and in a single afternoon, they can make all the plants in an area look like they were used for target practice.

People ordering plants online in the United States these days expect their plants to arrive Instagram ready—not a mark, scuff, or wrinkle is acceptable. But no outdoor-grown plant looks as perfect as its greenhouse-grown cousin, with or without ants. It is very difficult to produce and provide perfect plants when they are grown outdoors in the wind and rain and then shipped through the postal system. I'm actually amazed when a plant arrives in good shape!

CHAPTER TWO

Finding Extraordinary Plants

Plant collecting has really changed in the past few years. For example, two decades ago, when I first got into collecting, I was looking for unusual plants. Then I wanted variegated plants, and this somehow morphed into collecting mainly aroids and gingers. I met many people along my journey, and each person introduced me to other collectors who shared my passion for unusual plants.

Most collectors are extremely generous with both plants and information. Sometimes, when someone was reluctant to part with a particular plant, it was exciting for me when, after many visits, the collector would share a small plant with me. Back then, if I was lucky enough to be granted access to someone's collection, I learned not to touch the plants or take pictures until I asked first. I learned that not everything is for sale. When I visited a collector, I brought home tips on growing that I couldn't find on the internet, and I learned tricks firsthand from those experts who'd been growing plants for ages. In conversations, I found out who had a particular plant that I didn't know I needed yet. Many collectors had incredible stories to share about their adventures finding and acquiring particular plants. I recently spoke with an older collector who explained that he used to acquire plants by writing letters (with pen and paper) to botany professors in Central America, asking if they might know of someone growing a particular plant he was after or have access to seeds of a particular species he wanted to grow. They would send a letter back, and further correspondence would result. It could take months before he was successful in his quest.

It's much easier to find plants now than it used to be. We can check online plant auctions, access plant importers' lists, or ask fellow collectors to find what we're looking for. Your best bet for rare plants is generally to look online, unless you're lucky enough to live near a really great local nursery or plant shop that features interesting plants. A simple online or social media search for a plant often yields lots of great results. Auctions on eBay and collectors in Facebook groups can be great sources of plants these days, although some of the prices can be astronomical. Sales groups on Facebook ("Time to Splurge and Purge" is a good one) and some Instagram users have started to use their accounts to sell and share plants as well. An online search for a coveted plant should help you find what you're looking for. At the back of the book (see page 201), I've included a list of reputable growers and suppliers that have been around for years.

Importing Plants from Abroad

If you want to try legally importing plants from countries outside the United States, you can apply for an import permit online from the US Department of Agriculture Animal and Plant Health Inspection Service (USDA APHIS, see www.aphis.usda.gov). Permits for imported plants are free for individuals, usually with a pretty fast turnaround for approval. Of course, many regulations and requirements affect which plants you can import, where they can be imported from, how they must be prepared before shipping, and quarantining requirements.

Look for legitimate plant exporters with a simple Google search for the type of plants you are after. Your newly imported plants will need some time to acclimate, because they will be shipped after the surrounding soil has been removed, and they've often spent quite a bit of time in shipping, inspection, and quarantine. Importing can be incredibly stressful to plants because of delays and shipping damage. You, and your plants, are likely to go through some pain and suffering before plants arrive. They rarely arrive looking showroom ready.

Plant Meet-Up Groups

Check online to look for houseplant meet-up groups or clubs in your area. Members often enjoy getting together to swap plants and information. If you don't find a group, start your own. At the very least, these groups can be a great way to get to know people with similar interests. One of the best aspects of trading plants with others is that you can often obtain plants that might not ordinarily be for sale. Many of the collectors I know reserve special plants to use as trades for other sought-after plants that may not be otherwise available.

Buyer Beware

When something seems too good to be true, it usually is. Some online sellers may try to make a quick buck without providing quality goods, and this happens more than you might think. If there are no photos of the plant for sale, ask. Reputable sellers are usually happy to provide images of exactly the plant you're considering buying and if they won't, walk away. I've seen a lot of mislabeled plants and made-up hybrids selling on Facebook groups, and this makes my eye twitch. Stem cuttings and unrooted cuttings (see page 155) are fine to buy as long as they are fresh, but it's a shame to see already partially rotted pieces of plants being sold with black or brown rotted stems and no fresh growth points. If you're a beginner, you may want to avoid stem cuttings and unrooted cuttings altogether. Because they have no leaves, it's difficult to know what you're buying, particularly if you don't know what to look for.

If you're buying a plant online, it's usually pretty easy to determine whether your plant is coming from a reputable source. Ask for references, and do your research by looking for online reviews or by asking friends where they've obtained quality plants online. There are loads of great and trustworthy sellers online these days (see page 201 for some suggestions).

When trading plants online or in person, trade with a source you know well, or ask for references who can vouch for them. You don't want to ship off your plant and never hear from the other person again.

When buying plants at a nursery or plant shop, you should always try to choose full, compact, and thriving plants. Ensure that the soil doesn't have a sour or bitter odor—the potting media should smell earthy and natural (a lot of nurseries like to use cheap, peat-based soils to cut down on expenses if they are producing large quantities of plants). Check the soil and the plant for insect damage. If any other plants in the area are suffering damage from pests or disease, don't buy the plant, even if your selection looks good—you may not notice insect problems until after you take it home.

To help avoid buying poached plants, ask the seller where the plants originated. You want to know whether they are nursery grown or wild collected and if importing, that the seller can provide you with the proper paperwork for importing. You obviously don't want to contribute to the problem by buying wild-collected plants. It can be difficult or impossible to discern whether a plant has been wild collected just by looking at it. You can be sure, however, that cultivated plants such as variegated monstera and Pink Princess philodendron don't occur in nature and are therefore not poached; the same is true for any boutique plants or nursery cultivated hybrids. Some say that poached plants are easy to spot if they have stumps or large stems attached. Although this can be a tell-tale sign, some growers—myself included—create new plants using stem propagation methods when producing smaller-size plants.

IS IT REALLY RARE?

You hear the word *rare* tossed around quite a bit—maybe a bit too much. Some plants that are rare in cultivation may not be rare in nature, and some plants are critically endangered in their natural habitat but plentiful in cultivation, such as *Philodendron hastatum*. Sometimes the term is just used as part of a sales pitch. If you find one seller calling a plant "rare," it pays to look around at a few other sellers to confirm that it's true so you don't get taken advantage of or overcharged. By doing a thorough online search, you will get a better sense of overall prices and availability for a plant.

Consider Your Needs and Your Growing Environment

There is a plant for you no matter what your growing conditions are like. You just need to learn to work with what the plant wants. You can't fight nature, after all, so don't torture yourself or your plants trying to make them grow in unsuitable

Say No to Plant Poaching

Plant poaching is the illegal collection of rare and endangered plants from their natural habitat. When you buy plants that have been illegally collected from the wild, you create and sustain a market for unscrupulously collected plants and perpetuate the problem. Though it's always exciting to find something new, and prices for these plants may be cheaper than nursery-grown plants, buying wild-collected, poached plants is irresponsible. As long as people are buying poached plants, there will continue to be a market for them. The plants often never recover from being pulled from the ground, so not only have they been taken from their natural habitat, they often die once they're in your care. Often not enough plant material is left behind by poachers to support the remaining population, and entire localities of plants can be wiped out by a single collector. Don't buy poached plants. . . . Just don't. End rant.

spaces. They may not die right away in less than ideal conditions, but they will never look their best and thrive.

A good part of my success is related to choosing plants that prefer the growing conditions I can provide, and as a result, I suspect I like these plants because they grow well for me. (I don't like the ones that don't grow well for me nearly as much, but I assume they are just playing hard to get, so I keep trying.)

Working with the plant to give it what it needs is a lot easier than trying to force it to grow where it doesn't want to grow. Any plant will grow well if you can provide the proper growing environment. Is your home growing environment dark or brightly lit, dry or humid? To a limited extent, you can improve your environment using lights and humidifiers, which are covered in chapter six.

After you play with your plants' light, humidity, and watering needs (see "Watering" on page 166), consider grouping plants together based on their shared needs. If some plants require more water or more humidity, for example, group them together in one place to save time watering and caring for them.

LIGHT REQUIREMENTS

Before you decide where to place a plant, you need to know what type of light you have in your home and what type of light the plant prefers. There are three categories of light needs for plants: indirect light, bright indirect light, and direct light.

Indirect light This area isn't brightly lit and there is no direct light hitting the plant. There is only the natural light of the room with no supplemental lighting (see page 188). This is the least amount of light of the three options.

Bright indirect light The area is well lit by natural light, but the light is not shining directly on your plants. Bright indirect light is roughly equivalent to outdoor shade. This is the sweet spot for most aroids, including philodendrons, anthuriums, monsteras, and alocasias. Bright indirect light is the most versatile type of light situation, because even some plants that prefer direct light will tolerate it, such as variegated *Monstera adansonii* and *Philodendron lynamii*.

Direct light This refers to sunlight that passes directly through a window and shines on your plants, with nothing blocking the light. Direct light is preferred by monsteras and some philodendrons, although the velvety philodendrons, such as *Philodendron verrucosum*, *P. melanochrysum*, and El Choco Red philodendron (*P. triumphans* 'El Choco Red') prefer bright indirect light.

Note that "natural light" refers to sunlight coming in through your windows. Regular lightbulbs don't offer any benefits to plants, only full-spectrum LED or high output florescent lighting (see "Supplemental Lighting," page 188) can be useful.

Here are a few tips to make the most of the light within your home:

After you find the perfect spot with the best lighting for your plants, put up a plant shelf up so that you can group more plants together to enjoy the light.

Use hanging baskets, shelves, and wall-mounted planters to display your plants at different levels and take advantage of the light.

Generally, the closer plants are to a window, the stronger the light will be. If the light is too bright or you notice any leaf burn, move the plant a little farther away from the window.

Place a large mirror across from a window to help reflect the natural light and give you more plant placement options.

Notice how the light changes in your home throughout the day. It can also change quite a bit with the seasons. You may need to move plants as the light changes with the seasons. Plants that were previously in perfect lighting conditions may be getting brighter light than they prefer or no light at all.

HUMIDITY REQUIREMENTS

Humidity is the amount of water vapor in the air. It is life giving, especially for tropical plants. To determine the humidity level in your home, use a hygrometer, which you can purchase at a hardware store, nursery center, or online. Follow the package directions to test the humidity in your home. Most tropical plants prefer about 55 to 75 percent humidity for optimal growth. In the "Growing Environment" for the plants in chapter four, you'll see specific humidity requirements for certain plants. I consider low humidity to be 50 to 60 percent, average humidity to be 60 to 70 percent, and high humidity to be 70 to 80 percent.

It's best to keep your plants away from heating vents to avoid warm air directly blowing on them. Although most houseplants need to be warm, they certainly won't tolerate excessive dehydration caused by overheated air.

BUDGET AND TIME CONSIDERATIONS

Next, think about your budget. Some exotic houseplants are quite expensive these days. If you're new to growing houseplants, it may be a good idea to first start with an extremely common, easy plant, such as a zz plant (*Zamioculcas zamiifolia*), which you can read about in many other houseplant books. If you are graduating from entry-level plants to extraordinary plants like those featured in this book, consider starting with less expensive plants such as *Philodendron gloriosum*, Ring of Fire philodendron, or *Anthurium veitchii*.

Finally, consider the time you have to devote to your houseplants. Some difficult and high maintenance plants can be quite time consuming to care for. (You'll find the difficulty level for each plant in the plant recommendations in chapter four.) Most plants, however, are pretty low maintenance once you get their needs dialed in.

CHAPTER THREE

Your Plants Are Home. Now What?

If a plant arrives in a box, open it right away and carefully remove the wrapping and cushioning placed around the plant. I generally give new plants some water and a quick mist if they need it. Whether the plants arrived in a box or I picked them up from a local nursery, I like to think they appreciate a refreshing drink. (If the soil is already moist, however, the plant doesn't need more water.)

I also pinch or clip off yellow leaves. This greatly improves the plant's appearance and probably your state of mind. Yellow or torn leaves don't heal, and I like my new plants to put their energy into healthy green leaves. Plus, if there are damaged leaves on a plant, I'm more likely to be a helicopter plant parent and dote on the plant as if it were sick. Although it's normal for a few leaves to drop in the first few weeks after receiving a new plant, it can be scary. As long as the older leaves drop rather than the new growth, there's no need for concern. If you have a bright, humid spot, set the new plant there to perk up any drooping leaves. This is also a good time to look over the plant carefully for any pests (see page 190) that may have hitched a ride. Look at the back sides of the leaves and where the leaves attach to the stem, which are favorite hiding places for insects.

If you're picking up your new plants at a nursery, be careful as your transport your new family member home. Don't make it ride in the back of a pickup or hang its head out the window—the wind will shred all the leaves off! I'm not ashamed to admit that I've brought more than one plant home in its own seat, buckled in with a seatbelt. Luckily I've never been pulled over with a plant next to me wearing its seatbelt.

In the winter, tropical plants can even suffer cold damage in the time it takes to walk from the shop to your car. Be sure the plants are wrapped up before you leave the store with the leaves covered in either layers of paper or cloth.

In chapter two, you looked around your space, considered the available lighting, and hopefully acquired a plant that matches your lighting conditions. However, even if you bought a plant that prefers direct light, avoid placing it near intensely bright light for at least four or five days until it adapts to its new surroundings, especially if it's been wrapped up in a dark shipping box for a few days.

Many people have the urge to repot their new plant immediately. I usually don't repot new plants right away and prefer to give them a couple weeks to recover from a move, especially if they were shipped to me. (Imagine what the plant goes through when being shipped in a box—it's probably worse than a hurricane!) Some aroids, alocasias in particular, will completely hang their leaves until they've had a few days to readjust. I used to take alocasias to plant shows, and the poor plants' leaves would droop as a result of the truck ride to the show. After a couple days, they would spring back to normal, but by then the show would be over and it would be too late for them to have found a new home. (I suspect they were doing it on purpose because they didn't want to leave me. That's what I like to think anyway.) The trick is not to move a new alocasia for a few days after it arrives; after you're sure it has enough water and no insect pests, leave it alone for a while or its leaves will hang even more.

I normally don't fertilize plants when they first arrive. I figure they need a break from the stress of travel, so I usually wait a couple weeks to let them settle into their new home before I add anything other than water. (When it's time to repot and fertilize, consult the instructions on pages 178 and 170.)

Quarantining New Plants

Quarantining new plants for three or four weeks is probably a good idea if you have other indoor plants at home. It might seem like a lot of time, but insect eggs are difficult to see and take a while to hatch. Three to four weeks will be enough time for

you to notice whether the plant is suffering from disease or is harboring insects or their eggs. You don't want to introduce pests to the rest of your plants.

Pests can get out of control quickly in an enclosed indoor environment with little ventilation. Generally, it's best to quarantine your new plants in a separate room, or at least across the room, from the rest of your plants. If you don't have any rooms that aren't already full of plants, you can seal a new plant inside a clear plastic bag, like a terrarium. Don't give it too much light while it's in the plastic bag, because the bag will amplify the light and heat, which can damage the plant.

A few days after you place the plant in quarantine, check the backs of its leaves, down in the leaf axils where the leaves attach to the stem, and the soil in the pot for insects. Pop your plant out of the pot and do a quick inspection of the soil, being careful not to disturb the roots more than necessary. Put some glasses on if necessary or use a magnifying glass to spot any tiny critters moving about in the soil. If you notice any insects, you can apply insecticidal soap or neem oil, or carefully wash the leaves with soapy water.

If you take your plants outside in the warmer months, you risk bringing in pests with the plants when you bring them indoors again before the cold weather. It's still worth it to give your plants the fresh air, however, and they will reward your efforts with beautiful new growth. As with newly purchased plants, quarantining plants brought indoors for the winter is a good idea. When the quarantine period is over, check your plants again just to be sure they are pest free before you turn them loose with the others. Keep in mind that unhealthy or stressed plants are more likely to experience pest infestations. This may seem counterintuitive: wouldn't a pest prefer a nice lush, healthy green plant for lunch? The occasional pest is not the same as an infestation, however, and weak plants are prime targets for serious issues. Insects are normal outdoors, but we don't want them on our indoor plants. (See page 190 for more information on pests.)

Acclimating Plants to Their New Home

After you decide where the plant will be located, leave it in place for a couple of weeks to enable it to acclimate to its new home. During this time, it may lose a few leaves or appear stressed. Unless the leaf drop is excessive or the plant is losing new leaves, you need not be concerned, because this is normal; the plant was probably raised in a greenhouse in near perfect conditions, and you're asking it to get used to completely different lighting, less humidity, and different water quality. Once your new plant settles in and adds some new growth, it may be time to repot it, if necessary. (See page 178 for repotting information.) Try to resist the urge to move it to a new location unless you have determined that this spot isn't the best one for the new plant—perhaps the lighting isn't best, for example. If you keep moving it, it's difficult for the plant to continually acclimate to different locations with different light levels or humidity, and this will stress your plant.

CHAPTER FOUR

Fifty Extraordinary Plants

This list of fifty of my favorite and/or most requested plants represents a drop in the bucket of the many great aroids you can acquire. In this list, every plant is uniquely identified by its botanical name, which consist primarily of two parts: a genus name (such as *Anthurium*) and a species name (such as *forgetii*). Some plant names in this list include additional identifiers that refer to cultivar names (in single quotation marks), particular forms of the species, provisional names (indicated by ined., short for ineditus, meaning "unpublished" and cf., short for conferre, meaning it's waiting for botanists to confer and confirm), unknown species (indicated by sp.), or unofficial names (in parenthesis and double quotation marks).

Each plant offers some special features. Whether they are easy or difficult to grow, unusual, or just plain amazing, they all have a special place in my heart.

Each plant described includes level of rarity (in other words, how easy or difficult it is to find) and level of ease or difficulty involved in caring for it.

RARE indicates how easy or difficult it is to find the plant at online auctions or sales events (such as eBay and Facebook), at nurseries, from importers, from other collectors, at plant shows, and from other sources. The RARE levels of availability are as follows:

- **Easy to find (not rare)** At this level, plants are easily found with a simple Google search of online sites and auctions, or at plant shows, local nurseries, and plant shops.

- **Moderately easy to find (somewhat rare)** At this level, plants are sporadically available with an online search and occasionally at plant shows, local nurseries, and plant shops.

- **Moderately difficult to find (rather rare)** At this level, plants become harder to find. They are more rarely available online (but still possible to find) and most likely not in your local nursery or plant shop. Possibly found as an import.

- **Difficult to find (rare)** At this level, plants are hard to find; most likely it will take some work and research. You might find it as a trade or import.

Levels of **CARE** difficulty relate to the following factors:

- **Easy to care for** At this level, a plant is almost a "set it and forget it" plant. Once you put these plants in a good spot, they basically take care of themselves aside from watering and occasional fertilizer.

- **Moderately easy to care for** At this level, plants may need a bit of extra care, such as some extra humidity or supplemental lighting.

- **Moderately difficult to care for** At this level, plants require extra monitoring to be sure they're happy and their care is dialed in. They will most likely need supplemental humidity and lighting.

- **Difficult to care for** At this level, plants will definitely need supplemental humidity and lighting, and extra care should be taken with water quality. These plants are rewarding for people who enjoy a challenge and provide great bragging rights when you succeed, but they are known for being temperamental and making you question why you started trying to grow plants in the first place.

SECTION Section classification is useful in propagation for crossbreeding plants (see page 144).

GROWING ENVIRONMENT This indicates the quality and types of elements required in the plant's immediate environment, including light level (see page 25), soil constitution (see page 168), water requirements (see page 166), temperature requirements (see page 188), and suitability for planting on totems or in hanging baskets (see page 174). Humidity preferences (see page 26) are also included for three major levels: low (50 to 60 percent), average (60 to 70 percent), and high (70 to 80 percent).

Aglaonema pictum 'Tricolor'

This dwarf, multicolored plant looks as though it were painted in camouflage, with bright splashes of color adorning each leaf. It grows wild in the tropical and subtropical areas of Malaysia, Sumatra, and New Guinea but is found all over the world in private collections. Its relative ease of growth indoors makes it very popular with houseplant owners.

SECTION *Aglaonema*

RARE ● ● ●

When it is available, I usually see it at specialty plant shops, eBay auctions, and Facebook.

CARE ● ●

In general, it seems to be a pretty easy houseplant, but spider mites and mealybugs seem to find it delicious. Deal with them using insecticidal soap or neem oil.

GROWING ENVIRONMENT

It prefers bright indirect light, average humidity, and well-draining soil.

COLLECTOR'S NOTES

This aglaonema is usually easy to spot anywhere because its color patterns are so different from those of other plants. There are a few forms of this plant, some more robust and more colorful than others. I've imported them, but most of those plants just didn't have the color or vitality of plants already available from other US growers.

Alocasia cuprea

The rippled leaves of *A. cuprea* look as though they were hammered out of copper. This native of Borneo grows to 2 feet tall, but what it lacks in size, it makes up for in beauty. This is a wonderful shade-loving aroid that is simply not collected much these days.

SECTION N/A
(Alocasias don't have sections)

RARE ● ● ●

The availability of this plant keeps changing. Tissue-cultured plants were readily available at many south Florida growers, but then they seemed to disappear for a while. I haven't seen them offered much lately.

CARE ● ●

Medium difficulty. The biggest issue is rot; to avoid that problem, it must be planted in loose, well-draining soil.

GROWING ENVIRONMENT

This alocasia needs bright indirect light, average humidity, and well-draining soil. It definitely seems to prefer cooler nights—not cold, but in the high 60s to 70s Fahrenheit.

COLLECTOR'S NOTES

Alocasia cuprea was discovered in 1891 by Karl Koch on a routine expedition to the island of Borneo. I've seen photos of huge plants happily growing in the wild in Singapore, and I've seen the plants in captivity at Atlanta Botanical Garden and Missouri Botanical Garden, where they all were growing so well, I questioned whether they were the same little plants that I was growing. It just goes to show how aroids can look different depending on their age and their growing conditions.

Anthurium ×
'Ace of Spades'

You'll sometimes see 'Ace of Spades' abbreviated as AOS. This hybrid (as indicated by the × in its name) came out of Hawaii many years ago. Although no one seems to be sure of its exact parentage, everyone agrees that it is one of the most spectacular dark velvet anthuriums. Its nearly black, heart-shaped leaves are so dark that they appear translucent. New leaves emerge a chocolate brown color.

SECTION *Cardiolonchium*

RARE

May be available online on eBay or via Facebook groups.

CARE

Moderately easy. A pleasure to grow with the usual anthurium care (see "Growing Environment").

GROWING ENVIRONMENT

Bright indirect light and high humidity are important, as is well-draining soil.

COLLECTOR'S NOTES

'Ace of Spades' was being grown from seed and then via tissue culture, mostly at Silver Krome Gardens nursery in Homestead, Florida. I think many of us tend to overlook plants that are too easy to find, but I have appreciated my AOS for many years. I used to have a huge, mature plant that Bill Rotolante at Silver Krome gave me as a birthday present in 2004, until a hurricane ate it. It lived in my old collection shade house with a family of veiled chameleons.

Anthurium ×
'Dark Moma'
(aka "Dark Mama")

This gorgeous hybrid of *A. warocqueanum* (page 69) and *A. papillilaminum* (page 58) exhibits the best of both parents. Its leaves remind me of a stretched out *A. papillilaminum*. It's just beautiful! I occasionally have trouble growing both parent species because of the Florida heat. (Or my incompetence; maybe I just don't want to admit it.) This hybrid, however, grows with ease in my hot shade house, where it flourishes! This is a really nice plant. The hybrid was first created by the late anthurium breeder John Banta and then re-created by breeder Jay Vannini some years later. John is responsible for introducing and describing countless plants into the trade. He was not only a gifted grower, but he was also incredibly generous with both his plants and knowledge. You could ask him anything about plants and he knew the answer. I was lucky enough to visit him several times over the years and always came away having learned something new.

SECTION *Cardiolonchium*

RARE

I haven't seen it available much, but online auctions like eBay and Facebook plant groups are your best bets.

CARE

This is relatively easy to grow if given proper humidity and elevated to provide space for its long leaves.

GROWING ENVIRONMENT

This anthurium appreciates indirect light, high humidity, and well-draining soil. It's great for hanging baskets; when grown successfully, the leaves can get quite long, so they display best hanging or in a pedestal-shaped pot.

COLLECTOR'S NOTES

I first saw this hybrid under the name 'Dark Moma' and couldn't read the tag properly or assumed it was spelled wrong, so I started writing 'Dark Mama'—and the internet ran with it. Sorry, John. As a hybrid, the plants can vary quite a bit—some leaves may be greener and some may be longer.

Anthurium clidemioides

With pebble-textured leaves of only a few inches long, this cute and interesting vining anthurium from Costa Rica and Panama looks almost like it belongs in the *Piper* genus due to the heart-shaped pebbled leaves that many *Pipers* are known for. Its leaves can be nearly black in lower light conditions or a lighter green in bright light, which are so different that the two variations appear to be from two completely different plants. Plants with similarly textured leaves grow in low light areas that are consistently wet. It is believed that the texture helps capture light and shed excess water.

SECTION *Polyphyllum*

RARE ●●

Your best bet is online through a terrarium plant supplier.

CARE ●●●

Moderately difficult unless it's in a terrarium. Can be a slow grower.

GROWING ENVIRONMENT

This anthurium prefers indirect light, high humidity, and well-draining soil, and I find that it grows very well in a terrarium. It is also a great specimen for a totem; otherwise, it will ramble around, crawling across the table with extremely long, stretched internodes (distances between leaves) looking for something to climb on.

COLLECTOR'S NOTES

The first time I saw *A. clidemioides*, it was in the collection of Ralph Lynam of Davie, Florida, who grew his plant happily on a totem that had been rolled and coated in cement dust. He mentioned that it must be grown this way because in nature, it is found on limestone outcrops. I assumed it must be nearly impossible to grow, but years later, I saw a beauty in Mary Sizemore's collection that was crawling everywhere—under benches, into other pots, and up aluminum supports—with not a bit of limestone in sight.

Anthurium crystallinum

Anthurium crystallinum is many collectors' gateway to anthuriums. It's found in Central and South America, from Panama to Peru. With its heart-shaped, velvety leaves with silver veins, what's not to love? Occasionally, the plant's new leaves emerge in varying shades of red. For my plants, this coloring seems especially common in the winter.

SECTION *Cardiolonchium*

RARE

Usually easy to find via importers, eBay, or Facebook sales groups.

CARE

A nice, respectable, easy anthurium that you can bring home to your mother. Great starter plant that is also good looking.

GROWING ENVIRONMENT

Like most anthuriums, *A. crystallinum* prefers bright indirect light, high humidity, and well-draining soil.

COLLECTOR'S NOTES

Most *A. crystallinum* plants in cultivation are probably hybrids. They easily cross with many other species and have produced many bench hybrids, which are plants that result from seed that you didn't pollinate yourself and whose other parent is a mystery—though somehow your plant produced seeds. Think immaculate conception anthurium. Over the years, I've seen many plants labeled *A. crystallinum*, but most are hybrids.

Anthurium cutucuense

The trilobed leaves of this anthurium have a pebbled (bumpy) texture that reminds me of a chicken foot. (Now you can't unsee that. You're welcome.) As if that weren't cool enough, the leaf petioles are speckled with red. It climbs, it's rare, and it's awesome.

SECTION *Dactylophyllium*

RARE

I haven't seen it available for sale lately, but it's sometimes available online or from importers.

CARE

Of the fifty plants covered in this book, this one is the most likely to make you question your poor life choices. It's mean and vindictive and has a bad attitude.

GROWING ENVIRONMENT

This finicky anthurium likes indirect light, high humidity, well-draining soil, and temperatures below 75°F. It prefers lower night temperatures of around 65° to 70°F. Water it only with the tears of an angel, on Tuesdays, on a full moon, while standing on one foot and singing "Stayin' Alive" by the Bee Gees. Didn't I say it was finicky? Grow it in a terrarium or grow tent (you can purchase these online) for the best chance of success.

COLLECTOR'S NOTES

I've seen this anthurium grown skillfully in San Francisco in a private collection, at the High Elevation House of the Atlanta Botanical Garden, and in the wild in Ecuador. It still eludes me, however. When I saw it growing in Ecuador, it was so cold that I wore a jacket—but keep in mind that I'm from Miami, so anything below 80°F is a shock to my system and hurts my skin. (Brrrr! I feel cold just thinking about it.)

Anthurium forgetii

This species is highly variable. I have had plants with beautiful silver veining and some with almost no visible silver coloring at all. Although this Colombian native has been described since 1906, there is little information available about it. Most anthurium leaves feature an open sinus or space between the top lobes of the leaf where it joins the petiole (leaf stem), which creates a heart-shaped leaf. In contrast, *A. forgetti* is most easily distinguished by the closed sinus at the top of its leaves; its peltate (shield-shaped) leaf shape is almost round. The leaves of younger plants and seedlings can feature open sinuses, which can change to more typical closed sinuses as the plant matures.

SECTION *Cardiolonchium*

RARE
Generally available online through eBay or Facebook auctions.

CARE
Pretty easy but requires high humidity to do its best.

GROWING ENVIRONMENT
Prefers bright indirect light and high humidity. Well-draining soil and even watering is best. Like all anthuriums, *A. forgetii* likes water but doesn't like to sit in wet soil.

COLLECTOR'S NOTES
The leaves can be nearly black in color with more discreet venation or showier silver-veined versions, likely from a different locality or possibly a hybrid. My first *A. forgetii*, a gift from Marie Selby Botanical Gardens in Sarasota, Florida, had dark leaves. Many years after I received my plant, I noticed that leaves of imported plants from Ecuador were silver-veined.

Anthurium luxurians

The bullate (puckered) texture on the dark leaves of this anthurium is striking. I've created a few hybrids with this plant, but their leaf texture is not as striking as that of the parent plant, so I prefer the pure species. Endemic to Colombia, it is not in abundance, even in nature. This plant makes you do a double take and is one of my top five favorite anthuriums.

SECTION *Cardiolonchium*

RARE

Sporadically available online on eBay and Facebook auctions or from importers.

CARE

Midrange in terms of ease of growing. Not the hardest anthurium to grow, but not really an entry-level plant.

GROWING ENVIRONMENT

Indirect light and average humidity are the keys to growing this beauty. As with all anthuriums, well-draining soil is important, so make sure that the growing media is loose and light.

COLLECTOR'S NOTES

For many years, an elderly plant collector, Skipper Mize, used to come down to South Florida about once a year. He carried lots of cash strapped to his chest like a bomb. I've never seen anything like it, especially in South Florida. He mentioned that he had forty or so large *A. luxurians* plants. (I thought to myself, whatever . . . sure you do.) The following year, however, he invited me to visit his greenhouse in Orlando. Sure enough, the plants were placed in a row like a hedge along the floor of his greenhouse, with leaves of about 20 inches long. I'm still in shock just thinking about it. My original plant was a gift from Skipper. He purchased one plant from the now defunct Fantastic Gardens Nursery in Miami (sadly, it closed before my time, so I never got to visit). He had been propagating it from seed over the course of twenty years or so.

Anthurium offolteranum ined.

Anthurium offolteranum ined. is believed to be from northern Ecuador. Long, narrow, ribbed leaves hang down like those of *A. veitchii* (page 65), but *A. offolteranum* ined. leaves are more narrow.

SECTION *Belolonchium*

RARE   ● ● ● ●

As of this writing, this plant is not yet available but as soon as the official name is published, importers will be your best bet.

CARE   ● ●

This plant hasn't been particularly difficult to grow, but it hasn't broken any speed records either, which leads me to believe it prefers a bit cooler environment than I am offering it. In the sweltering heat of Miami, indoor growers have an advantage over those of us who grow outdoors.

GROWING ENVIRONMENT

This plant appreciates indirect light, average humidity, and well-draining soil.

COLLECTOR'S NOTES

In an exciting development, this plant is being provisionally named in my honor for my work with the International Aroid Society (IAS) by Tom Croat of the Missouri Botanical Garden (hence the ined. designation, which indicates a provisional name, yet it's strangely similar to my first name). The official naming description can't be established until my plants produce an inflorescence, which they are in no hurry to do. An inflorescence and leaves are needed to preserve as herbarium specimens. What better honor than being a plant person and having a plant named after you? Can you think of anything better? I'm waiting (tapping foot impatiently).

Anthurium papillilaminum

This plant really is one of the most beautiful of the dark, velvet-leaved anthuriums. It is endemic to Panama, where it grows on steep slopes at lower elevations. The stretched out shapes of its leaves make *A. papillilaminum* look a bit different from any of the more common heart-shaped velvet anthuriums.

SECTION *Cardiolonchium*

RARE ● ● ●

Importers, online auctions such as eBay, and Facebook plant groups are your best bets.

CARE ● ●

Not the easiest to grow, but not a drama queen either.

GROWING ENVIRONMENT

Provide indirect to bright indirect light. Like many of the velvet-leaved anthuriums, it needs high humidity and well-draining soil.

COLLECTOR'S NOTES

I first saw this beauty at collector Dewey Fisk's nursery many years ago. Though a few different forms are available, the quilted veined, dark-leaved clone 'Fort Sherman' is my personal favorite. This plant is totally worth growing. It took me years to get my first *A. papillilaminum*, and when I think about how difficult it was to get these plants when I started out, I almost can't believe my good fortune. Now more people are growing them from seed, which is wonderful, but it has become difficult to find the pure species with so much natural hybridization going on.

Anthurium regale

This plant is surely deserving of its royal name, and it is one of a few anthuriums that leave you absolutely speechless. Hailing from low elevations in Peru, it has been a successful grower for me. Big dark leaves with white veins are the hallmark of this beauty.

SECTION *Cardiolonchium*

RARE

Importers, eBay auctions, and Facebook plant groups are your best bets.

CARE

Anthurium regale can be a little picky about the lack of humidity indoors and weather that's a bit too cold . . . or hot. Or it has a headache.

GROWING ENVIRONMENT

Anthurium regale appreciates bright indirect light, high humidity, and well-draining soil. If it's happy, it can grow quite large, so give it a good amount of space.

COLLECTOR'S NOTES

I had never seen *Anthurium regale* in person (or in plant) until the 2002 IAS show, when Betsy Feuerstein motioned for me to follow her. Under the table of one of the vendors was a collection of clear plastic cups topped with other cups, like mini greenhouses. (Hint: this is a pretty cool way to grow small aroids—see page 152.) Inside the cups were little *A. regale* plants. Until then, I had seen this plant only in a photo with Dr. Mardy Darian on the Exotic Rainforest website (www.exoticrainforest.com).

Anthurium rotolantei

Although this species is most likely from western Colombia, no one seems to be 100 percent sure where it originates. The pebbled leaf texture resembles that of *A. cutucuense* (page 50) or a slightly watered down version of *A. luxurians* (page 54).

(page 50) ... (page 54)

SECTION *Polyneurium*

RARE ● ● ● ●

This extra nice plant isn't readily available, but it may be acquired through online auctions at eBay and Facebook plant groups. You might find it online from other collectors for trades.

CARE ●

Very easy to grow. This has been a very unassuming grower for me.

GROWING ENVIRONMENT

Provide indirect light, high humidity, and well-draining soil.

COLLECTOR'S NOTES

Anthurium rotolantei is named in honor of Denis Rotolante of Silver Krome Gardens in Homestead, Florida. He and his son Bill are the premier aroids growers in the United States. Interestingly, I have repeatedly tried to convince mine to set seed—once with *A. warocqueanum* (page 69) as the pollen parent and once with another *A. rotolantei* as the pollen parent. The *A. warocqueanum* cross produced loads of fruit, but I found only two seeds in all of them and then misplaced the seedlings. The *A. rotolantei* × *A. rotolantei* cross was also full of fruit, but all of it was without seed— not a single seed at all. Dewey Fisk used to have an *A. rotolantei* in his collection that had come from Fairchild Tropical Botanic Garden. I had gazed longingly at one of these plants at Fairchild for years. One day, tired of seeing me drool on their plants, the garden staff mercifully gave me a cutting, and I lived another day to write this book.

Anthurium veitchii

Anthurium veitchii, the king anthurium, is native to the departments of Antioquia and Chocó in Colombia, where it grows epiphytically on trees. Although this species has many forms, you will often encounter the wide and narrow forms, which refer to the distance between the ripples, or pleats, on the leaf rather than the width of the leaf itself. Plants that grow in different localities will show mild differences in leaf shapes and sizes.

SECTION *Calomystrium*

RARE

Relatively easy to acquire. Often available from online sellers and occasionally at plant shows.

CARE

Relatively easy. Definitely not a starter plant, but not terribly finicky in the appropriate light, humidity, and soil conditions.

GROWING ENVIRONMENT

This anthurium prefers indirect light, average humidity, and well-draining soil mix with lots of added horticultural charcoal and orchid bark. Anthuriums do not tolerate soaking wet soil, which can easily rot their roots. Most wild-growing anthuriums with pendulous leaves grow on hillsides or epiphytically on a host plant. This is a great plant to grow mounted on a totem or in a hanging basket, with potting media and moss packed around the roots, to provide ample room for the long, quilted leaves to hang down.

COLLECTOR'S NOTES

I acquired my first *A. veitchii* from the great collector Dewey Fisk, at a time when this plant was very difficult to find. It was infested with mealybugs, whiteflies, and spider mites—the pest trifecta! Although Dewey didn't want to sell it because he intended to deal with the insects first, I begged him to let me buy it until he relented. (I can be very annoying . . . er, persuasive.) He made me promise to put the plant inside a garbage bag in my driveway and treat it there so that the insects would not spread to other plants in my collection. It survived the infestation, but I eventually managed to kill the poor thing by messing with it and repotting it five times until it just couldn't take any more abuse. Visiting Dewey was my first experience with someone who was growing lots of aroids. He had several cobbled together shade houses, where he grew a conglomeration of plants that interested him. If ever there was a character, it was Dewey. On my first visit, he greeted me at the gate in his standard uniform of tiny green shorts, no shirt, and a sweat rag tossed over his shoulder. At the time, he had compiled a wonderful online plant list to help with identifying aroids, because it seemed there were very few aroids in cultivation in the United States at the time—or maybe I just didn't know where to look back then.

Anthurium villenaorum

From Peru, *A. villenaorum* has crisp, unusual, triangular shaped petioles (leaf stalks) that grow downward, with leaves like folded wings. Although easy to grow, my plant is not breaking any speed records adding new leaves. Its slow growth makes it likely that it will probably never be very common in cultivation, though it's one of my favorite anthuriums.

SECTION *Cardiolonchium*

RARE

Sporadically available these days from importers, eBay, and Facebook groups.

CARE

These plants are pretty easy to grow.

GROWING ENVIRONMENT

Anthurium villenaorum grows best in bright indirect light, high humidity, and well-draining soil.

COLLECTOR'S NOTES

When a friend introduced me to this plant at a show, I was ecstatic over its perfectly triangular stems. (I'm apparently easily amused.) Because of its hanging, folded leaves, this anthurium is a great for a hanging basket. It is cute for sure, but it can be frustrating to package the plant for shipping because its leaves do not want to fold up over the plant. I've crossed *A. villenaorum* with the true *A. besseae* and the offspring were quite disappointing—they looked like *A. besseae* plants that had been stepped on.

Anthurium warocqueanum

Also known as the queen anthurium (or by the nickname warocq), this velvety beauty comes from Colombian rainforests and grows epiphytically, hanging from trees or cliffs. Its dark leaves can grow to 4 feet long when the plant is thriving. This is a variable species, with some plants featuring green leaf surfaces and some with leaves so dark they appear black.

SECTION *Cardiolonchium*

RARE

Can be moderately difficult to acquire. Occasionally available at plant shows and sporadically available from online vendors.

CARE
Tricky, high maintenance, sadistic diva of a plant that does its best to make you cry. Needy, temperamental, and will spontaneously die, just when you thought you had it all figured out. Not generally a good introduction into aroids. (I'm actually sweating just thinking about it.) If you can grow this plant, you have arrived, and you can grow anything . . . or you're a witch.

GROWING ENVIRONMENT
Prefers indirect light to bright indirect light, high humidity, and well-draining soil amended with lots of orchid bark and horticultural charcoal. Hanging baskets are best for large warocqs. When you are successful growing her, the queen can grow quite large and needs lots of room for her velvet leaves to hang down.

COLLECTOR'S NOTES
I purchased my first *A. warocqueanum* at a plant show as a new import, bare root, in a bag. I raced all the way home with the air conditioning blasting in the car because I had heard that they do *not* like heat. But as soon as I took it out of the plastic bag, it collapsed. It did eventually recover, somewhat, but later died.

Anthurium warocqueanum × rugulosum

I simply cannot say enough about this hybrid. The long, thick, leathery leaves have an unusual corrugated texture. I'll step out on a limb and say that I think that this hybrid is better looking and an easier grower than either of its parents.

SECTION *Cardiolonchium* (*A. warocqueanum*) and *Polyneurium* (*A. rugulosum*)

(However, I don't know anyone who has gotten seeds on this plant—sometimes hybrids like this can be sterile.)

RARE ● ● ●

I haven't seen it available much lately, but online auctions like eBay and Facebook plant groups are your best bets.

CARE ●

Not fussy at all. This awesome plant can grow quite large. I find it impossible to grow *A. rugulosum* long term here in South Florida—and by long term I mean twenty-four hours. Luckily, for some reason, this hybrid grows wonderfully for me.

GROWING ENVIRONMENT

This hybrid requires indirect light, high humidity, and well-draining soil.

COLLECTOR'S NOTES

A juvenile *A. warocqueanum* × *rugulosum* is difficult to tell apart from an *A. rotolantei* (page 62). As it matures, the hybrid's leaves grow more elongated and develop a matte surface that is more pronounced than that of *A. rotolantei*. I first saw this plant in Hawaii in the late collector Karel Havlicek's collection. I'll bet the leaves were more than 30 inches long. In fact, Karel had a pure *A. rugulosum* so large that I didn't even know what it was at first, since I had never seen a leaf longer than 6 inches before that time. In 2017 when I last visited Hawaii, I saw some of these for sale at the local Home Depot, of all places. It seems a local grower was selling off his excess plants, which were labeled "10-inch Tropical Foliage."

Anthurium wendlingeri

This native Costa Rican may have one of the most unique inflorescences around; it spirals like a spring, more so as the plant matures. It's absolutely incredible! The leaves resemble pleated crushed velvet and can be up to 7 feet long in the wild. Who doesn't love that? Many of us need a cold shower after seeing an anthurium like this one.

SECTION *Porphyrochitonium*

RARE

Sporadically available online and from plant groups on Facebook.

CARE

Relatively easy, once established. No crazy demands. An acceptable plant for a beginner to a moderately knowledgeable plant grower.

GROWING ENVIRONMENT

Bright indirect light and average humidity are important. I've found that most of the anthurium species with pendulous leaves prefer well-draining soil. They seem to do best if their rhizomes and aerial roots are not buried too deeply in the planting media. They are good candidates for hanging baskets.

COLLECTOR'S NOTES

My first big *A. wendlingeri* came from a collector who was liquidating his collection. I had never met this plant in real life and only seen pictures of it before I purchased this one. It was thirty-five years old when I purchased it, and now it's fifty. It was broken in half a few years ago by someone who may or may not be buried in my back yard. The other half of it is living its best life at the Fairchild Tropical Botanic Garden's Rare Plant House in Coral Gables, Florida.

Monstera adansonii
white (aka "albo") variegated form

Some plants are popular for seemingly no reason, but that is not the case with *M. adansonii* variegated form. It is a truly beautiful plant. Likely a sport from Japan, the variegation is the mutation. The green-and-white-striped petioles are just as beautiful as the leaves. A few other variegation patterns are starting to show up on the scene, but I prefer this form.

SECTION *Monstera*

RARE ● ● ●

Easier to find than it used to be but can be on the expensive side. Facebook, eBay auctions, and specialty plant shops are the best places to look for it.

CARE ● ●

Easy to moderate. May require a bit of extra humidity. The white parts of the leaf may brown if the humidity is below average.

GROWING ENVIRONMENT

This plant prefers bright indirect light, high humidity, and well-draining soil. A totem will give it something to climb and the support it needs to grow larger leaves.

COLLECTOR'S NOTES

New leaves may emerge as half white and half green—I've seen this referred to as "half moon" variegation. The plant can display several different color patterns: there are a few varieties from Thailand with gold-colored rather than white variegation and other white-variegated forms from Indonesia. This is another ultra-expensive plant that I split the cost with a friend to afford it (see page 101), but it was totally worth it. We were some of the first growers to bring it into the United States, but others soon followed suit. Within a few years, this plant has been added to many collections.

Monstera
'Burle Marx's Flame'

This aroid has so much going for it—beauty, ease of growth, and it's just so weird looking! With deep and irregular fenestrations (perforations), its leaves can look skeletonized. Burle Marx's Flame is so interesting that it startled me the first time I saw it.

SECTION *Tornelia*

RARE   ● ● ● ●

This crazy-looking monstera is not readily available. But if you do find one, it's usually from an importer, though occasionally you'll see one listed in auctions on Facebook or eBay.

CARE   ● ●

Easy to medium. Most monsteras like this one are really forgiving, they can take whatever you throw at them in terms of light and humidity.

GROWING ENVIRONMENT

This plant likes indirect to bright indirect light, average humidity, and well-draining soil. Give it a totem or other support for climbing to get the best growth and mature leaves.

COLLECTOR'S NOTES

This plant was introduced to the trade as *M. dilacerata* until botanists declared that the species name was incorrect. Because it was found growing in the Rio de Janeiro garden of the late Roberto Burle Marx, and no one knows where he collected it originally, botanists have found it difficult to determine its proper species.

Monstera deliciosa

white (aka "albo") variegated small form
(formerly M. borsigiana)

This plant has many color variations, and most of them carry colloquial names such as "Half Moon," "Mint," and many more. Most of the available variegated white monsteras are variations of *M. borsigiana* (the former name, not used much anymore, but you will see it used occasionally), which don't grow as large as the standard *M. deliciosa*, but they are still beautiful.

SECTION *Monstera*

RARE

Pretty easy to find these days online but the price has gone through the roof. (You can't see me, but I'm rolling my eyes.)

DIFFICULTY

Does very well indoors; however, white areas of the leaf may turn brown, especially if humidity is less than 65 percent.

GROWING ENVIRONMENT

Provide bright indirect to direct light, average humidity, and well-draining soil. Use a sturdy totem for best growth.

COLLECTOR'S NOTES

White variegated monsteras caused plant hysteria and became one of the most popular plants around, mostly because of beautifully styled Instagram images. I was not prepared for the onslaught of requests. Even now, plant influencers' Instagram pages are packed with pictures of perfectly grown variegated monsteras. Believe it or not, this used to be a $30 plant at wholesale nurseries; now one plant can command thousands of dollars. (Even at $30, I'd be shocked and would walk away—$30 for a plant? Why, whoever heard of such a thing?)

Monstera dubia

This is another neat plant. The variegated juvenile form is so vastly different from the mature form that you would swear they were two completely different, unrelated plants! When young, this super cool aroid grows flat against its climbing structure, with overlapping leaves, like shingles, that have silver markings. I love the way it shingles when attached to a climbing surface. As it grows to maturity, it sends out large, perforated adult leaves that are completely green.

SECTION *Marcgraviopsis*

RARE

I see these pop up from time to time at auction on eBay and Facebook pages and at specialty plant shops. Check terrarium suppliers.

CARE

Easy to mid-range. This monstera is a pleasure to grow.

GROWING ENVIRONMENT

Monstera dubia prefers bright indirect light, average humidity, well-draining soil, and a totem or other suitable climbing host so it can grow larger leaves and shingle. Otherwise, its leaves will be tiny and it will scramble around searching for something to climb.

COLLECTOR'S NOTES

To me, the most interesting thing about *M. dubia* is the complete transformation of the juvenile shingling leaves to mature leaves. Its juvenile leaves often resemble those of *Rhaphidophora cryptantha*, making proper identification difficult. Fairchild Tropical Botanical Garden used to grow *M. dubia* and *R. cryptantha* side by side, climbing together. Many discussions occurred in front of those plants, trying to discern which plant was which. Although I find it difficult to confuse the two, their young leaves do have similar silvery markings.

Monstera obliqua

The most well-known form of *M. obliqua* is from Peru, and this seems to be the one that has gained popularity. With its delicate, heavily fenestrated, lacy leaves, this monstera has caused something of an internet sensation the past couple of years. In 2020, it became sort of a status symbol when images of the plant flooded social media. It is occasionally confused with *M. adansonii* by the uninitiated, but the Peru form of *obliqua* is much more hole than leaf. Unscrupulous sellers will sometimes try to sell the more common *M. adansonii* as *M. obliqua* to make a quick buck.

SECTION *Monstera*

RARE

Facebook groups, eBay, and specialty plant shops are the best places to look for it. Can be very expensive.

CARE

Moderately easy but will suffer without high humidity.

GROWING ENVIRONMENT

It needs bright indirect light, high humidity (consider a terrarium), and well-draining soil.

COLLECTOR'S NOTES

This dainty monstera doesn't climb like some others do. Instead, it sends skototropic (light-avoiding) runners slithering along the ground, making offsets. The demand for *M. obliqua* has become pretty intense with people even selling and growing the runners. Palm Hammock Orchid Estate in Miami used to have loads of these monsteras growing on its greenhouse benches. Then someone brought a tray of them in 4-inch pots to the IAS Aroid Show and sold them for $8 each. I remember picking one up, looking at it, thinking, "Hmmm . . . I think I have this . . . yawn," and then putting it back.

Monstera standleyana

white (aka "albo") variegated form

This plant has such bright and beautiful variegation. The usual all-green form is native to Costa Rica, and its oval leaves climb when grown on a totem, or it can easily be grown in a hanging basket. So many aroids grow huge, but this one stays a reasonable size. Mine haven't attained any leaves more than 8 inches long.

SECTION *Monstera*

RARE

This plant is becoming more accessible from mainstream sources, and I've occasionally seen it at nurseries, plant shows, and on eBay and Facebook auctions.

CARE

Easy. Monsteras make great houseplants, and *M. standleyana* is no exception.

GROWING ENVIRONMENT

Bright indirect light, average humidity, and well-draining soil are important. It displays best on a totem, or you can trim off sections to make the plant fuller and plant the cuttings in a hanging basket.

COLLECTOR'S NOTES

There are a few forms: all green, which is the naturally occurring form; aurea, or gold, variegation; and albo, or white, variegation. I had the white variegated version of this plant for years before I discovered the gold form. I still can't decide which one I like the most.

Philodendron × joepii

A possible natural hybrid (as indicated by the × in its name), *P. × joepii* (pronounced "YOOP-ee-eye") has been on every serious plant collector's must-have list for years. As the plant matures, its leaves go through an incredible transformation, with each leaf shape and variation crazier than the last. This philodendron is nearly extinct in the wild and was found by naturalist Joep (pronounced "Yoop") Moonen more than twenty years ago during an ecological tour of the Maroni River in French Guiana. After an exhaustive search, he found only one additional plant; it is believed that fewer than four plants remain in the wild. This philodendron was originally introduced to the United States at the IAS Annual Aroid Show many years ago. There is really nothing quite like this aroid, and the exaggerated bottom leaf lobe gives character and interest to this climbing philodendron. The leaf shape is at its most dramatic when the plant is in its "teenage" years and not yet fully mature.

SECTION *Schizophyllum*

RARE

Sporadically available online in eBay and Facebook auctions.

CARE

Easy grower, but can be a little cold sensitive if it's growing outdoors. (Ask me how I know. On second thought, don't.)

GROWING ENVIRONMENT

Bright indirect light is best, with average humidity and well-draining soil. This is a great philodendron to grow on a totem, which will help its leaves grow larger and more interesting. This plant likes it warm and prefers the temperature to be above 60°F.

COLLECTOR'S NOTES

Upon discovering this plant for the first time, Joep Moonen (for whom the plant is named) initially thought the leaves had been chewed by leafcutter ants because of their strange, uneven edges. After I had searched for this philodendron for many years, Joep handed me one at an IAS show—just like that. Poof! I had *P. × joepii*.

Philodendron ×
'Pink Princess'

If you love bright, gaudy, variegated leaves, this is the plant for you. Splotches of hot-pink variegation cover its new leaves. Talk about brightening up your living space! Pink Princess is believed to be a *P. erubescens* hybrid. Because it has reddish leaves, where no dark pigment exists it shows as pink rather than white as it would be on a green leaf. It seems to have brighter colors for me in the spring.

SECTION N/A
(Often hybrids don't have assigned sections if the parents are unknown.)

RARE

Available online via eBay and in Facebook groups but should be easy to Google and find in online shops and in local nurseries as well. It's usually more expensive than is reasonable.

CARE

Pink Princess is easy to grow in moderate humidity.

GROWING ENVIRONMENT

Pink Princess needs bright indirect light, average humidity, and well-draining soil. It does best on a totem.

COLLECTOR'S NOTES

I hesitated to include Pink Princess on this list because it's not necessarily a rare plant, but it has become so popular in the past few years that I decided it deserved to be here. Most growers were tossing this plant in the mulch pile a few years ago. Suddenly, however, it was the hottest thing going, and we were all left scrambling, trying to find some to grow. Pink Princess is a bit too "bubblegum" for my taste—although I appreciate how it brightens up an indoor space, I don't care for its unnatural look in the garden.

Philodendron billietiae
variegated form

A large-growing, variegated philodendron, this
P. billietiae (pronounced billy-ET-ee-ay) shows intensely
colorful variegation and bright orange petioles. I love
it—it's like a rainbow. However, the leaves tend to revert
back to green if I fertilize the plant, which I think is kind
of ungrateful. The pure green form of *P. billietiae* is from
French Guiana and was discovered by Belgian botanist
Frieda Billiet in 1981. The variegated form is most likely
a sport (a genetic mutation) that came from Thailand
and was selectively propagated.

SECTION *Macrobelium*

RARE   ● ● ● ●

The usual place to find this plant is an
importer out of Thailand. Occasionally,
however, someone may have already
imported it and will make it available
on a Facebook auction or sales page.

CARE   ●

This plant gets big when it's happy,
and it's pretty easy to keep happy.

GROWING ENVIRONMENT

Bright indirect to direct light, average
humidity, well-draining soil, and ample
space are needed. This plant can
stretch to 5 feet wide. A sturdy totem is
important for support and best growth.

COLLECTOR'S NOTES

I acquired my first variegated *P. billietiae* at the IAS show. It was tiny
and smashed, but I bought it anyway. I do that more often than I'd
care to admit, but I feel obligated to save these plants! It recovered
and added a couple green leaves, with no variegation. Now, however,
the variegated leaves of the single plant hang over the rest of my
collection in the greenhouse.

Philodendron 'Burle Marx's Fantasy'

This miniature climber (whose leaves grow to about 6 inches long) is thought to be or be related to either *P. hopkinsianum* or *P. ushanum*. Popular in the terrarium trade, its ease of culture and overlapping, appressed growth habit (leaves are flat and close to the stem) make it easy to identify. It was discovered in the garden of the late Brazilian landscape architect Roberto Burle Marx.

SECTION N/A

(This species has not been assigned to a section. No one has bloomed it that I know of, and botanists need an inflorescence to properly assign a section.)

RARE

An often overlooked source for this philodendron—or any of the other small philodendrons in this list—are plant businesses in the terrarium trade. It is pretty common in the terrarium trade, so if you're looking for it, check with terrarium plant suppliers.

CARE

A good beginner plant that's perfect for a totem. It takes a while to get established and get down to the serious business of growing, but once it starts, it grows easily indoors.

GROWING ENVIRONMENT

This plant likes bright indirect light, average humidity, and well-draining soil. Because of its small size, this is a great terrarium specimen. When climbing, its interesting, overlapping, almost shingling (overlapping leaves cling to the support structure) growth habit is easy to appreciate. While you may not get to see it grow to its full potential in a small terrarium, in a taller enclosure you can really enjoy it.

COLLECTOR'S NOTES

If grown without a totem, this little philodendron will have much smaller leaves with long internodes (distance between leaves) while it scrambles, looking for something to climb—not a good look. Grow it on a totem to encourage growth of full-sized leaves. The first time I saw this plant was at collector Ralph Lynam's little greenhouse, where he kept the good stuff. He had one plant that was shingling up a tree fern totem and I instantly fell in love with it.

Philodendron esmeraldense

The leaves of this gorgeous climbing philodendron look as if they were made of leather, and each new leaf grows larger and darker. It is most abundant in the Esmeraldas Province of Ecuador, but it has a widespread range throughout Ecuador and Colombia. Because it naturally grows in relatively low elevations (at least by Ecuadorian standards) of between 1,400 and 3,600 feet, it has been a treat for me to grow in Florida. Plants that naturally occur in higher elevations generally require cooler, super humid conditions that I can't provide and that are difficult to re-create indoors. When happy, this one can get really, really big.

SECTION *Philodendron*

RARE ● ● ●

I haven't seen *P. esmeraldense* offered much lately, but I have seen it occasionally at large orchid shows.

CARE ● ●

This plant is a bit cold-sensitive when grown outdoors and starts to suffer when temperatures drop to around 45°F.

GROWING ENVIRONMENT

Philodendron esmeraldense does best with bright indirect light, average humidity, well-draining soil, lots of space to grow, and a totem or other climbing host.

COLLECTOR'S NOTES

I've always thought that *P. esmeraldense* looked like sort of a wider leaved *P. patriciae* (page 122). It has a similar constitution, similar growth habit, and the leaves have a similar leathery texture. While visiting Ecuador, I noticed that the leaves of these philodendrons varied from very wide to quite narrow, especially on mature plants.

Philodendron fibrosum

Described (named and cataloged) in 2010, this philodendron species occurs in Colombia and Ecuador at 2,460 to 6,230 feet. Its heart-shaped leaves are beautiful, but its fuzzy petioles are the best. This is a very interesting aroid.

SECTION *Philodendron*

RARE ● ● ●

Importers, online auctions on eBay and Facebook, and private collectors can be good sources.

CARE ● ●

Relatively easy, but needs high humidity to be truly happy.

GROWING ENVIRONMENT

This philodendron does best with bright indirect light, high humidity, and well-draining soil, with a totem for support.

COLLECTOR'S NOTES

This plant reminds me of a round-leaved *P. serpens*. It seems to be a variable plant that may have super hairy (squamous) petioles or sparse hairs on the petioles, akin to those on a fly. (Am I the only one who's seen a close-up of a fly?) My first plant, which had the sparsely haired petioles, was a gift from Atlanta Botanical Garden. Years later, I acquired another form whose petioles had far more fuzz, like a shag carpet. I can't decide which one I like best.

Philodendron 'Florida Beauty'

This philodendron has fiddle-shaped green leaves, splashed with creams and white. It's really incredible! It's easy to see why it would grab your attention, with the pattern of variegation on the leaves in varying degrees. This has long been one of my favorite variegated philodendrons.

SECTION *Schizophyllum*

RARE

Available online, from eBay and Facebook groups, and in specialty plant shops.

CARE

Easy, although white leaf areas may brown in indoor conditions, especially in low humidity.

GROWING ENVIRONMENT

Provide bright indirect light, average humidity, and well-draining soil. Use a totem for best growth and display.

COLLECTOR'S NOTES

This is one of the first philodendrons I ever grew. Miami's now-closed Palm Hammock Orchid Estate used to have a Florida Beauty philodendron that was so large that the plant spread across the nursery benches. It could never be sold, because it was basically a huge mound of leaves that would need to be propagated first. Florida Beauty plants have been in and out of my collection several times.

Philodendron 'Florida Ghost'

Because only a few people are growing Florida Ghost, this gorgeous white-leaved philodendron is not commonly seen in collections. New leaves are bright white, fading to a lime green as they mature. My favorite thing about this philodendron is that its leaves may appear in both colors on the same plant. This is especially noticeable during the growing season.

SECTION *Schizophyllum*

RARE ● ● ●

Only occasionally available online via eBay and Facebook groups.

CARE ● ●

Its white leaves can drop in low light or wet conditions. With a lack of chlorophyll, I suppose it needs all the help it can get.

GROWING ENVIRONMENT

Florida Ghost prefers bright indirect light, average humidity, and well-draining soil. The only issue I've had with Florida Ghost is that the white leaves may melt, or drop, if the soil is kept too wet or the light is insufficient. A totem or other climbing surface is important for this climber.

COLLECTOR'S NOTES

The first time I saw Florida Ghost, it was being offered on eBay by collector Dave Gordon. Dave had all things variegated and was a wealth of information. It was routinely selling for more than $200, an outrageous price for a plant at the time. So a friend and I decided to buy it together. We cut it in two and the rest is history. We debated about how the plant would fare, worried that the small cutting wouldn't root or that the remaining, rooted plant would die. But both parts lived and grew up strong and healthy.

Philodendron gigas

From the Panamanian lowlands, *P. gigas*, my friends, is certainly the Cadillac of philodendrons! As if it being chock-full of dark, velvety goodness wasn't enough for the discerning aroid collector, this plant can grow to an enormous size. In fact, in optimal rainforest conditions, mature plant leaves can be more than 4 feet long and 3 feet wide. It may be troubled by pests, but the extra care you take is absolutely worth your time. Did I mention its big, dark, and velvety leaves?

SECTION *Philodendron*

RARE

Specialty plant shops, eBay, and Facebook auctions are the most common places to find this plant.

CARE

Can be picky, like most of the velvet-leaved philodendrons, unless it has high humidity and successful pest control.

GROWING ENVIRONMENT

This plant prefers indirect light, high humidity, and well-draining soil. Its leaves can be quite large as the roots attach and climb, so a sturdy totem is a good idea.

COLLECTOR'S NOTES

Discovered in Panama by Dr. Thomas Croat of the Missouri Botanical Garden, *P. gigas* leaves can be difficult to tell apart from those of *P. melanochrysum* (page 121) when juvenile, but *P. gigas* quickly grows much larger and darker than the latter. I often wonder what goes through someone's mind when they see a philodendron like this for the first time in situ, with 4-foot-long, black, velvety leaves. Swoon! Chris Hall of Equatorial Exotics in Australia pollinated her *P. gigas* plants years ago, and most of the plants in cultivation in the United States now are likely from her original work.

Philodendron gloriosum

This philodendron is one of the most beautiful Colombian aroids and has been highly sought after for a couple of years, with no sign of diminishing demand.

SECTION *Philodendron*

RARE

Should be easy to acquire online on eBay, in Facebook sales groups, or in specialty plant shops.

CARE

Relatively easy. Take a little extra care to check for pests or keep the humidity high, because it may be susceptible to spider mites in an environment with lower humidity.

GROWING ENVIRONMENT

Provide indirect to bright indirect light, high humidity, and well-draining soil. There's no need for a totem, since the plant crawls along the surface of the soil. Keep the plant's rhizomes above the soil line, because they prefer to run along the surface of the soil; burying them too deeply can cause them to rot. In fact, most of the philodendrons with creeping growth habits should be planted with their rhizomes above the soil line.

COLLECTOR'S NOTES

Philodendron gloriosum is available in a few different forms, which probably originate from different localities. I've seen plants with intense seashell-pink coloring on the backs of their leaves, and a few grow much larger and rounder than others. This philodendron tends to have darker leaves in lower light that become lighter green with more light. At the now-closed Palm Hammock Orchid Estate in Miami, *P. gloriosum* grew in a huge clump in a greenhouse that had an evaporative cooler to keep the temperature down. The plant's pot had tipped over and it had climbed out and was growing over the concrete pathway. So much for the perfect soil mix!

Philodendron gloriosum
white (aka "albo") variegated form

This has been an easy grower for me, though maybe not as simple as the more common all-green *P. gloriosum* because of its delicate white leaf sections. But its beauty makes up for any extra drama.

SECTION *Philodendron*

RARE   ● ● ● ●

Virtually nonexistent in cultivation. Only a couple growers in Florida and Thailand are growing this plant, and all are offsets of a single original.

CARE   ● ●

Relatively easy, but white sections of the leaf may turn brown.

GROWING ENVIRONMENT

This plant prefers bright indirect light, average humidity, and well-draining soil.

COLLECTOR'S NOTES

If any plant could look more like a butterfly, I don't know what it would be. It was a sport (a genetic mutation) from a normal green *P. gloriosum*. A few new leaves emerged with white variegation, those sections were propagated, and the rest is history.

Philodendron gloriosum × melanochrysum 'Glorious'

This fantastic hybrid was created by gifted Australian hybridizer Keith Henderson. I have owned one for years and have always admired it. To the untrained eye, it looks remarkably like a wider version of *P. melanochrysum* (page 121) with rounder leaves. In fact, when the plant is young, it is difficult to tell the two apart; when this velvety hybrid is mature, however, stand back—it grows larger than *P. melanochrysum*.

SECTION *Philodendron*

RARE ●●

Much easier to find these days than it used to be. Look for it online in Facebook sales groups, eBay, and specialty plant shops.

CARE ●●

Easy to medium difficulty, but needs the right humidity and temperatures.

GROWING ENVIRONMENT

Provide indirect light, high humidity, well-draining soil, and warmer temperatures (70° to 80°F). A totem is important for support and to encourage large leaf growth.

COLLECTOR'S NOTES

My original plant came from the late, great collector Dewey Fisk. After taking up hours of his time asking questions, I saw this philodendron rambling around on his greenhouse bench and up in the rafters. When I stopped to admire it, he said it was *P. andreanum*, a name that was thought to be synonymous with *P. melanochrysum* at the time. He rolled his eyes, grabbed a fistful of the philodendron, and said, "Take it kid, and go!"

Philodendron heterocraspedon

Philodendron heterocraspedon looks superficially like *P. patriciae* (page 122) when it's young, but as it matures, it develops narrower ripples down the entire length of the long, narrow leaves. The first time I saw this jaw-dropping Colombian philodendron I was blown away and knew I would die without it. Luckily I got one … whew!

(page 122)

SECTION *Philodendron*

RARE ● ● ● ○

Online vendors and importers are your best bets to find this philodendron. I haven't seen any offered in a couple years at a reasonable price, since it doesn't seem to be imported or propagated as much as it used to.

CARE ● ○

Can be a bit cold sensitive if it's kept outside.

GROWING ENVIRONMENT

This plant requires bright indirect light, average to high humidity, and well-draining soil. Use a sturdy totem for best growth.

COLLECTOR'S NOTES

I haven't been growing *P. heterocraspedon* for long, but my plant seems to be doing well, although it's not breaking any speed records for growth. I imported this plant as an unnamed species based on the description alone, and I knew what it was immediately when it arrived based on pictures I had seen online. I prefer to buy plants online when they are properly named, but I'm also not one to ignore a beautiful plant just because it hasn't been named yet (undescribed) or because the seller doesn't know what it is. This is another philodendron I thought I'd never have the opportunity to grow, since I didn't know anyone growing it. After acquiring this plant, a friend was so enamored with its beauty that he actually got a tattoo of the leaf on his arm.

Philodendron longilobatum 'Lelano Miyano'

SECTION *Schizophyllum*

RARE ● ● ●

Occasionally sold online on eBay and Facebook auction groups.

CARE ●

Easy, big, robust grower without a care in the world.

GROWING ENVIRONMENT

Provide bright indirect light, average humidity, and well-draining soil. A big climber, it benefits from a sturdy totem. This plant has a heck of a sideways spread, so give it some space.

This is a way cool Brazilian philodendron that was named for artist and naturalist Leland Miyano, who received it from his mentor, the late Brazilian landscape architect Roberto Burle Marx. With its big "ears" (leaves) that look as though they were cut with scissors, this philodendron is totally unique. Or maybe it's a little reminiscent of *P. × joepii* (page 86). Like *Anthurium forgetii* (page 53) and *Monstera dubia* (page 81), this aroid changes its leaf shape dramatically as it matures. Juvenile leaves go from a narrow *T* shape when young to a large, much wider leaf with serrated edges. Juvenile plants seem to be easily confused with Golden Dragon philodendron. I much prefer the juvenile leaves on *P. longilobatum*.

COLLECTOR'S NOTES

My first plant came from Leland many years ago, and later it became available from other sources as well. This plant can spread. I had one growing on a tree, and it eventually had a "wingspan" of at least 6 feet that blocked my pathway. (I did not think that out beforehand.)

Philodendron cf. lupinum

This philodendron occurs in two places: the Maynas province of Peru and in Amacayacu National Park, near the city of Leticia, Amazonas Department, in the south of Colombia. Young plants have velvety, dark, heart-shaped leaves that are red on the undersides. As they mature, the leaves become hourglass shaped with more of a matte texture. You'd swear they were two separate plants.

Originally to be named *P. vannini*, it may undergo a name change because there seems to be some confusion over whether *P. lupinum* and *P. vannini* are the same plant, so stay tuned.

SECTION *Philodendron*

RARE ● ● ●

Occasionally available online via eBay and Facebook groups.

CARE ● ● ●

Moderately difficult indoors but easy in terrariums.

GROWING ENVIRONMENT

This plant prefers indirect light, high humidity, and well-draining soil. A tall totem does wonders for support and lets you experience the huge changes this plant undergoes as it matures.

COLLECTOR'S NOTES

This lovely philodendron has been growing in my care since 2005, when I received it from my friend Jay Vannini (it was originally set to be named *Philodendron vannini* in his honor). Strangely, while we were assuming the plant wasn't in cultivation in any other collections, one of my friends in Thailand offered the plant to me. He had it labeled *P. micans*. I'm trying to figure out how this plant was already being grown in Thailand.

Philodendron luxurians

There are some plants I thought I'd never be lucky enough to grow, and this is absolutely one of those plants. Because this philodendron was listed in the old *Exotica* book (the *Exotica Pictoral Cyclopedia of Indoor Plants*, by Alfred Byrd Graf) as "Philodendron Choco," you may see it occasionally referred to as such. This tiger-striped, velvety aroid has an iridescent sheen to the leaves. Incredible! Said to be from the department of Chocó in Colombia, this is arguably one of the most beautiful philodendrons in my collection. It has a creeping habit similar to *P. gloriosum* (page 105), and it crawls along the ground in its native habitat.

SECTION   *Philodendron*

RARE

Occasionally online sellers will offer this plant, but you're most likely to find it in online auctions on eBay and Facebook.

CARE

Can be difficult to obnoxiously difficult. It's tricky to grow, particular if the humidity isn't high enough.

GROWING ENVIRONMENT

Indirect light, high humidity, and well-draining soil are important.

COLLECTOR'S NOTES

I had seen a black-and-white photo of this fantastic philodendron in the old *Exotica* book. I had no idea how beautiful this plant really was. Imagine my surprise when I saw it for the first time in full Technicolor. I was having trouble growing this philodendron and thought I had finally found the secret—it seemed to like wet soil, very little light, and a very well-draining soil mix. I called a friend who had been having trouble with his plant too. He said, "I'm glad you called. I found that *Philodendron luxurians* really likes to be bright and dry in a heavy soil mix!" So this just goes to show you, there's more than one way to skin . . . er, grow a philodendron.

Philodendron lynamii

Philodendron lynamii is endemic (native) to Tarapoto, Peru. The calling card of this big philodendron is its heart-shaped, hot-pink new leaves, which makes the plant quite collectable and in high demand. As the leaves harden off and mature, they turn a glossy olive green.

SECTION *Philodendron*

RARE

I have never seen this plant for sale at plant shows, but I have seen it offered on eBay and Facebook auctions.

CARE

Very easy to grow. Awesome plant that brings joy to all who grow it.

GROWING ENVIRONMENT

This philodendron prefers bright indirect light (a bit more light than anthuriums), average humidity, and well-draining soil. A crawler like *P. gloriosum*, it will eventually jump its pot as it grows sideways. At that point, repot it closer to one side of a larger pot, giving the growth point more room to spread across the pot.

COLLECTOR'S NOTES

This beautiful plant was named in honor of Ralph Lynam, who first collected it in 1981. He was a plant collector, tropical fish breeder, and Dewey Fisk's business partner. He was full of colorful stories. He once told me he credited his longevity to drinking a gallon of milk a day. He was ninety-eight years old when he passed away in 2010, so he must have been doing something right. This plant is a prime example of why it's so important to share plants with friends. After I lost my last *P. lynamii*, a good friend was wonderful enough to send me a piece from his collection, and all my resulting plants are clones of that piece.

Philodendron melanochrysum

Philodendron melanochrysum is found in the departments of Chocó and Antioquia in Colombia, from sea level to 500 feet in elevation. This is good news, because plants that grow at lower elevations are usually easy to grow indoors, while those from higher elevations require cooler temperatures and high humidity that are difficult to provide indoors. The leaves glitter slightly in the sunlight. Perhaps that's why it's named *melanochrysum*, which means "black gold."

SECTION *Philodendron*

RARE

Occasionally available through eBay and Facebook groups and at specialty plant shops.

CARE

Medium difficulty, prone to spider mites and mealybugs.

GROWING ENVIRONMENT

Indirect to bright indirect light, high humidity, and well-draining soil are important. Leaves will get much larger if it has a sturdy totem to climb.

COLLECTOR'S NOTES

This is easily one of my favorite philodendrons. It's simply a good-looking plant. The old Palm Hammock Orchid Estate in Miami had gorgeous and huge *P. melanochrysum* plants growing in its greenhouse. It's always startling to see such a huge, well-grown plant. This philodendron needs a protected environment to produce perfect leaves and is difficult to grow outdoors without suffering leaf damage. A shade cloth can help to keep falling leaves and debris from damaging its delicate leaves.

Philodendron patriciae

Of all the beautiful philodendrons in the world, *P. patriciae* may be the most striking of them all. When well grown, it can stretch 3 to 4 feet in length. It's from the department of Chocó in Colombia and when it first showed up in cultivation, it was informally called *P. splendidum* by Dr. Thomas Croat of the Missouri Botanical Garden, who is one of the world's leading experts on Araceae. When he later realized that a philodendron by that name already existed, he named this new plant for his wife, Patricia.

SECTION *Philodendron*

RARE ● ● ● ●

Harder to find these days, but you can occasionally buy them from importers or find them on eBay or Facebook groups.

CARE ● ●

Medium difficulty, it's a bit cold sensitive. Don't let the temperature drop below about 65°F.

GROWING ENVIRONMENT

This plant enjoys bright indirect light, high humidity, and well-draining soil. It needs a sturdy totem for climbing support.

COLLECTOR'S NOTES

Brian Williams of Brian's Botanicals and I used to email photos of this previously unobtainable philodendron back and forth, and we both dreamed about owning this plant for years. We would lament that we would never be able to grow it. How could we? This plant was not in cultivation at the time, it was found only in Colombia, and alas, we were in the United States . . . sigh. Then in the early 2000s at the IAS Annual Show, I was digging through a vendor's boxes, helping set up for the show, when suddenly I saw one. I carefully pulled it out of the box and searched the crowd for Brian. As soon as he saw my face, he knew something big had happened and he appeared next to me as if by magic. After he saw the plant, we may even have shed a tear together.

Philodendron 'Ring of Fire'

Philodendron 'Ring of Fire' is a great plant that adds interest, color, and texture to your indoor garden. The variegation on this climbing philodendron shows up as creamy white, white, and sometimes slightly pink, and leaves have interesting saw-tooth edges. It's most likely a hybrid of unknown origin.

SECTION N/A

(Often hybrids don't have assigned sections if the parents are unknown.)

RARE

Check online nurseries, specialty plant shops, and eBay and Facebook auctions.

CARE

Ring of Fire is a tough plant that is forgiving of inexperienced growers and can accept a wide range of care. It does fine in different lighting and humidity levels and isn't picky about growing conditions at all.

GROWING ENVIRONMENT

Provide bright indirect light bordering on direct light, average humidity, and well-draining soil. When the plant is young, you can make do without a totem, but as it grows larger, a totem provides support and the plant will grow larger leaves. It seems to show better color on new growth and with brighter light.

COLLECTOR'S NOTES

What is now called the Caramel Marble philodendron used to be called Ring of Fire. Then a flood of imports of this plant were brought into the country under the name Ring of Fire—and just like that, its name changed. I used to consider Ring of Fire as a kind of watered down replacement for Caramel Marble, something to settle for if you couldn't find the latter, but now I've grown more attached to it with each new, brightly colored leaf. I appreciate that the variegation never reverts back to green like the leaves of Caramel Marble sometimes do.

Philodendron rubijuvenile

(aka "El Choco Red")

This velvety aroid also has an iridescent sheen to its leaves. Incredible! Said to be from the lowlands of western Colombia, it is arguably one of the most beautiful philodendrons in my collection. It had no proper name when I acquired it, but the tag read *Philodendron* 'El Choco Red'. Young leaves are red on the reverse, but they lose that color entirely and become green as the plant grows and leaves mature.

SECTION *Philodendron*

RARE

Importers, large plant shows, eBay auctions, and Facebook are usually the best places to find it.

CARE

Some of the velvet-leaved philodendrons can be difficult to grow if humidity is too low (under 65 percent). The velvety leaf surface may make it more susceptible to spider mites, perhaps because there are more crevices and places for pests to hide.

GROWING ENVIRONMENT

Indirect to bright indirect light seems to be best. It likes high humidity and well-draining soil. It's a climber, so a sturdy totem is a great addition.

COLLECTOR'S NOTES

I've had this gorgeous philodendron since it stowed away in an import order as a *P. verrucosum* (page 134). I immediately grabbed it out of the box and gave it a special place on the climbing wall in the greenhouse. In retrospect, this was not the best spot for it, because it has climbed over to the door and is trying to escape outside of the greenhouse. I have to fight my way in and out the door now.

Philodendron serpens

Although the leaf surfaces of this philodendron are nothing to write home about, the petioles are covered in squamules (dense hairs), which may protect the leaves from predation from insects or channel water to the plant. I grow this plant solely for this unusual feature.

SECTION *Philodendron*

RARE ● ● ● ●

Availability seems to wax and wane since production seems to depend on the whims of the nurseries producing them, and often if the suppliers have a run on a particular plant, it may take them awhile to build up stock again.

CARE ● ●

Midrange. Seems to prefer a bit more humidity if grown indoors and is tasty to pests, especially mealybugs, which hide in the fuzzy petioles.

GROWING ENVIRONMENT

Bright indirect light, high humidity, and well-draining soil are required. It also needs a totem for support.

COLLECTOR'S NOTES

What we know as *P. serpens* may actually be a yet undescribed species, or it may be *P. squamicaule*, but originating at a different locale. To me, the two species have different growth habits and appearance—*P. squamicaule* is much more upright, its squamules have a different texture (more velvety than the dense hairs of *P. serpens*), and they are red rather than the pinkish blush of *P. serpens* squamules.

Philodendron sodiroi × verrucosum 'Majestic'

This cultivar has the silver coloring of *P. sodiroi* and the iridescence of *P. verrucosum* (page 134). It's always difficult to capture just how beautiful this plant is in a picture. The undersides of the leaves are red when the plant is young, but the leaves gradually lose the red coloration as the plant matures and climbs.

SECTION *Philodendron*

RARE

You can usually find it on eBay and in Facebook groups and auctions.

CARE

Easy to midrange. Sometimes hybrids have what they call "hybrid vigor," where the hybrids will grow better than either parent. This hybrid seems to be easier to grow than its parent *P. verrucosum.*

GROWING ENVIRONMENT

This hybrid needs bright indirect light, high humidity, well-draining soil, and a totem for support.

COLLECTOR'S NOTES

This is a great hybrid. I'm not entirely sure why it gets so large. Hybrid vigor? I haven't had either parent get even a quarter of the size that this hybrid has achieved. I owned this plant for years without knowing what it was. The hybridizer was Keith Henderson of Australia, who also hybridized *Philodendron gloriosum × melanochrysum* 'Glorious' (page 109).

Philodendron spiritus-sancti

This is it, guys—THE plant everyone wants to grow. Some love it for its beauty and some love it because it's the rarest of the rare. It is endemic to Espírito Santo, Brazil, near the town of Domingos Martins. Very few plants are believed to remain in the wild after being poached to such an extent that it's now considered to be endangered; most living plants are held in private collections these days.

SECTION *Macrobelium*

RARE ● ● ●

Whew! This is a plant that went from being hard to find and expensive to being a little easier to find and ridiculously expensive. It's now being produced by tissue culture in Thailand, so look for this rare plant to become more available in the future. Check auctions on Facebook and eBay.

CARE ● ●

This philodendron seems to prefer less humidity and more light than most other philodendrons.

GROWING ENVIRONMENT

It grows best in bright indirect light, low to average humidity, and well-draining soil. It doesn't require full sun or desert conditions, just a bit more light and less humidity than other philodendrons prefer.

COLLECTOR'S NOTES

This philodendron is hard to find, and though it may be a bit more available lately than it has been in the past, it is astronomically expensive. I used to know every collector who owned one—there were five of us. Then suddenly seed-grown plants were being imported to the United States from Brazil and everyone who had them in the United States started propagating like mad. The next thing you know, social media was awash in beautifully styled photos of them. The first plant I acquired I had sourced for a friend. By the time it arrived, however, he had already found one. So I kept it. Later, he asked to buy it because he wanted a backup plant, but it was too late. It had already grown two new leaves and I was smitten.

Philodendron verrucosum

The heart-shaped leaves on this beautiful South American philodendron can become huge, with a dark, velvety sheen that is unparalleled in the plant kingdom. The backs of the leaves show a wine-colored flame pattern, and the petioles and inflorescences are extra fuzzy, covered in squamules.

SECTION *Philodendron*

RARE ●

You can find it at specialty plant shops, plant shows, and online shops.

CARE ● ● ●

This plant is difficult to grow indoors because it requires higher humidity than most philodendrons (70 to 80 percent). I'd have to give it at least a medium to difficult. I stopped propagating it because it seemed like most of the plants I was shipping out were meeting with unfortunate endings after they arrived at the buyers' homes because of its humidity needs.

GROWING ENVIRONMENT

Provide indirect to bright indirect light, high humidity, well-draining soil, and a totem for climbing and support. This is a great terrarium specimen because it loves the extra humidity.

COLLECTOR'S NOTES

This philodendron is quite widespread throughout Central and South America and varies greatly by locality, with variable leaf size, amount of squamules, and degrees of red coloration on the reverse sides of the leaves. I had a difficult time acquiring this plant after I first became aware of it, but now I have six or seven forms of it under benches, growing up walls, and popping up in other plants. I saw *P. verrucosum* growing on the side of the road in Costa Rica, like a weed. Sadly, in the same area the next day, they had all been cut to the ground unceremoniously with a machete to tidy up the side of the road.

Rhaphidophora foraminifera

This plant can look very dramatic growing up a totem or another climbing structure. A native of Borneo, Sumatra, and Peninsular Malaysia, it is a large climber with elongated leaves. Its leaves change quite a bit from their juvenile form to climbing, mature leaves: young leaves have no fenestrations (holes and splits), but as it finds a climbing host, the leaves quickly lengthen and develop unique fenestrations on either side of the midrib for their entire length.

COLLECTOR'S NOTES

My friend and fellow aroid collector Mick Mittermeier saw this plant the first time in 2017 on an Instagram post from Erik van Zuilekom, an Australian living wall designer and plant expert. Erik found the plant while exploring Borneo and was amazed at its similarity to monstera. Mick had never seen it in the United States, and to his knowledge, it didn't exist in cultivation here. Mick consulted with Peter Boyce, the leading expert on the aroids of Peninsular Malaysia, and learned that it was easy to find in Malaysia and could be imported to the United States, but for whatever reasons, that never panned out. A few months later, I was able to import some from a Thai collector, and this was the plant's introduction to US cultivation. So far, it has proven to be a very hardy aroid with higher cold tolerance than most Bornean species, and it seems to enjoy brighter light than other rhaphidophoras. A white (aka "albo") variegated form is starting to become available in the United States, and I'm actually after it myself!

SECTION N/A

(Rhaphidophoras don't have sections.)

RARE

I've seen this plant offered in plant groups, and mine came from an IAS show a few years ago. You can occasionally find it as an import. It should start becoming more readily available, though, because it is such an easy grower.

CARE

Easy grower, forgiving of neglect. The leaves will curl if it gets too dry and will reopen once it absorbs moisture.

GROWING ENVIRONMENT

Provide bright indirect light, average humidity, and well-draining soil. I have *R. foraminifera* growing on a foxtail palm in my garden and up a support post in my living wall shade house. It appears to grow anywhere I put it, but the one in the shade house has a bit larger leaves and seems happier.

CHAPTER FIVE

Propagating Extraordinary Plants

One of my favorite things to do with plants is to make more of them! What's more magical than that? It's so much fun to experiment with different ways of propagating and everyone has their own preferences. A lot of people like to use water culture to root cuttings, while others prefer to use sphagnum moss or soil. In nature, most seeds don't get the chance to germinate because they are picked off by hungry critters or the conditions aren't quite right but when we plant them ourselves, we can be sure they have the best chance at growing into beautiful houseplants. Making more plants is an inexpensive way for you to expand your indoor jungle, a great way to produce extra plants to share or trade with others, and an interesting opportunity to crossbreed different plants and create something totally new.

Propagating from Seed

Plants, including aroids, produce flowers, which are pollinated and then produce fruit and seeds. In the wild, bees and other nectar-seeking insects usually transfer the pollen from the stamen (male part) of a plant's flower to the pistil (female part) of the same or another plant's flower, where fruit and seeds will be produced. But even plants in a greenhouse can be pollinated by wild creatures. I've seen a few surprising pollinators visit my anthurium flowers, including fruit flies, snails, and beetles, and I've seen lizards drinking the stigmatic fluid—they also like to bask on a plant's spadix (the fleshy spike of tiny flowers). Even though it probably isn't the lizard's intention, he may pollinate flowers as he moves around and carries pollen from one flower to another.

Otherwise, and especially if you want to cross two specific plants, you have to pollinate the flowers yourself to produce seed. Some plants are self-pollinated and include both organs on a single perfect flower, and these plants may or may not need a pollinator's help to produce seed. If you cross two plants of the same species, or if a plant self-pollinates, the plant will produce seed that can be used to grow new plants of that same species. If you cross two plants of different species, the seed produced will grow into hybrid plants that are a mix of the two parent plants.

All fifty plants in this book can be propagated from seed, but cuttings and other forms of vegetative propagation (such as cloning) are more common because they are faster. Propagating by cuttings creates exact copies of the parent plant, but seedlings (even if both parents are the same species) will vary a bit due to natural mutations. For that reason, setting seed among the same species is a great way to increase diversity of the species. Some of the seed-grown plants will be more robust than others, some will grow larger, and some may be more suited to your particular growing conditions. For example, it's difficult for me to propagate both *Anthurium warocqueanum* and *A. papillilaminum* from seed in the summer here in South Florida. Anthuriums generally don't like the heat, and most prefer a temperature drop at night. But I have a hybrid of the two, *A.* 'Dark Moma', originally created by John Banta and repeated by Jay Vannini, that grows like gangbusters!

When choosing plants to cross, think about how you can create a hybrid that surpasses either parent in some way. I choose to cross plants that I think will produce something more attractive or at least very different from the parents. I haven't always been successful, though. I created a hybrid of *A. besseae* and *A villenaorum* a few years ago that was disappointing ... and by disappointing I mean really ugly. This was the first time I realized that maybe I shouldn't make a cross just because I could. I recently had the option of crossing *A. dressleri* (super awesome, black velvet leaf) with *A. carlablackiae* (super awesome, black velvet leaf with white veins) but decided to set seed on each species separately instead. The prospective hybrid just didn't seem like much of a stretch from the intended parents.

POLLINATING ANTHURIUMS

When people see one of the big, leafy anthuriums in my collection, they often ask, "Does it bloom?" Of course it does! Although most foliage anthurium inflorescences are nothing to write home about (except the corkscrew blooms of *A. wendlingeri*), all anthuriums flower, and this is how they reproduce. A few species produce sterile (seedless) hybrids—for example, any offspring produced in a cross with *A. radicans* will be sterile.

The flowers on an anthurium are nearly microscopic in size and are produced on a spadix inflorescence. The female parts of the spadix mature first, followed by the male parts a little later, where pollen is produced. You can tell that the female parts are ready to accept pollen when tiny droplets of stigmatic fluid appear on the spadix. Female flowers are usually receptive to pollination for only a day or so after flowers open—this period is referred to as anthesis. Occasionally, a bit of heat is associated with this event—this is called thermogenesis. Often a scent is also associated—sometimes lemony, sometimes floral, and sometimes hard to describe. The scent is produced by pheromones that would normally attract specific pollinators, such as beetles, flies, and bees—or it could attract you. If your plant is fragrant, you can be sure that the inflorescence is in the mood to accept pollen. (*Yoo-hoo, boys! Over heeere!*)

Once the spadix is covered in stigmatic fluid (see photo, page 142), you need to gather fresh pollen from another inflorescence as soon as pollen is visible as white power on the spadix. Use a small paintbrush to brush the fresh pollen onto a small piece of folded wax paper or aluminum foil. Then brush or rub the pollen onto the receptive spadix with as much coverage as you can muster, which helps ensure an even seed set. If you miss a section of the spadix, that section won't produce seed. Transfer the pollen for a couple days in a row if possible to ensure that you get it done within the anthesis period. Then cover the spadix with a net bag or a pantyhose sock and use a twist tie at the top to secure it. This will keep curious pets or pests from eating your seeds. It's a good idea to write the pollination information on a label and add that to the inflorescence that received the pollen. Believe me, you won't remember what pollen you slapped on which plant six months down the road, especially if you are making many crosses.

One of the main roadblocks to successful pollination happens when the two inflorescences of the plants you want to cross are not ready at the same time—in other words, one of the inflorescences has produced pollen, but the other isn't ready to accept it. To avoid this dilemma, you can freeze the pollen of a plant to ensure that it's available to place on the inflorescences of the other plant whenever they become receptive. Use a paintbrush to brush the fresh pollen onto piece of aluminum foil, fold the foil over the pollen, label it with the name of the plant it came from, enclose it in a zip lock freezer bag, and then put it in the freezer. It will stay viable in the freezer for up to two weeks.

Sometimes, your efforts will produce unique and special anthuriums, but occasionally plants from different sections will not successfully cross, much to my annoyance. (I mean, we all need a velvety-leaved *A. veitchii*, right?) I try to keep an open mind, though, because I have nothing to lose by trying. Bill Rotolante from Silver Krome Gardens is constantly crossing plants that aren't supposed to be crossable, and he makes some great F1 (first-generation) hybrids and F2 (second-generation) crosses.

Oddly, many of my most mature anthuriums seem to self-pollinate nearly every time they flower, or maybe they're pollinated by a mysterious visitor when the lights go down. Until the resulting seeds are planted and grown, it's impossible for me to tell whether pollen I meticulously applied "took," or whether the plant simply self-pollinated again. (The cynic in me wonders about all those little plants that were eaten by snails or succumbed to fungus. I wonder if they were all successful hybrids that I'll never get to see.)

The first indication that your pollination attempt was successful will be tiny bumps, which will become future berries, that form along the spadix of the mother plant (see photo, page 143). If pollination hasn't been successful because of bad timing or expired pollen, the spadix will turn yellow and eventually fall off. It can take many months (and *A. clarinervium* can take up to two years) for these little berries to form. This is when you can determine whether your pollination efforts have borne fruit—literally. After the berries have formed, the inflorescence is considered an infructescence. Mature berries can be red, purple, orange, yellow, red, white, or even occasionally green when ripe. Usually the berry color is similar among plants belonging to the same section. The berries don't generally change color until they start to ripen a bit, but keep an eye on them as they ripen so you don't lose them as they fall off. Occasionally, I'll put a pantyhose sock or mesh bag over them so I don't lose them in the gravel—this also keeps animals from snacking on them.

Crossbreeding with Sections

Sections are typically used to help organize very large genera, which may include hundreds of species. In a large genus (such as *Anthurium*), a section groups together species that share certain similarities (such as *A. forgetii* and *A. warocqueanum*, which both have velvety leaf surfaces). Section classification is useful in propagation for crossbreeding plants to create hybrids: plants from the same section cross readily, while plants from different sections can be difficult to cross because they are too different genetically. The plants profiled on pages 38 to 137 contain section classifications to help you choose which plants will most successfully breed with each other.

POLLINATING PHILODENDRONS, AGLAONEMAS, ALOCASIAS, MONSTERAS, AND RHAPHIDOPHORAS

Pollinating a philodendron and species of *Aglaonema*, *Alocasia*, *Monstera*, and *Rhaphidophora* is a little trickier to accomplish than pollinating an anthurium. On the spadix, the male and female flowers are separate, with the male flowers at the top of the spadix and the females at the bottom, enclosed by the spathe even when the spathe is open for pollination. I have found that a plant is fertile and receptive to pollen when the spathe first starts to loosen (see photo opposite, top left). Once you notice that the spathe is completely open, you may have already missed your window of opportunity for successful pollination. (They are generally ready for pollen in the middle of the night, so get out your headlamp if you're an outdoor grower.) Gently wrap your hand around an inflorescence to check for heat; inflorescences produce heat and become fragrant when they are ready to be pollinated, in an attempt to attract pollinators, which may include fruit bats, beetles, flies, bees, and occasionally hummingbirds.

If you have frozen pollen from a separate inflorescence, grab it from the freezer. You may be lucky enough to have several inflorescences at different stages of readiness, and this is optimal. When pollen is visible as fine white powder, it is ready to use for pollination. (The methods for collecting and freezing pollen are the same as for anthuriums, see page 141.) Mix the pollen with a bit of water to make a paste. This makes it more manageable and helps with coverage. Cut away the spathe so you can access the female flowers (see photos opposite, top and bottom right), and use a paintbrush to paint or smear on the pollen paste (see photo opposite, bottom left). That's it. Walk away and wait.

HARVESTING SEEDS

Harvesting seeds from anthuriums is slightly different as compared to the other plants in this book, but I will discuss both methods here.

When anthurium seeds are ripe, the berries will pop partially out of the spadix (see photo, page 145). Don't force them out, if they haven't popped, they aren't ripe. With the other types of plants mentioned in this book (philodendrons, aglaonemas, alocasias, monsteras, and rhaphidophoras), the seeds don't pop out like an anthurium, but instead are surrounded by the fruit. When the infructescence has the consistency of a ripe banana, the seeds inside the fruit are ripe and ready for harvest.

If you accidentally snap the infructescence off of the plant (been there), depending on what stage they are in development, the berries or fruit may still ripen a bit more. Just put the snapped off portion somewhere safe (away from hungry animals and pets) to see if it puts any more energy into making seeds.

For anthuriums, remove the little berries from the infructescence. After you remove the berries, pop out the seeds by gently squeezing the berries. You can wipe off the slimy seeds using a paper towel, or rinse them in a fine strainer. I wipe

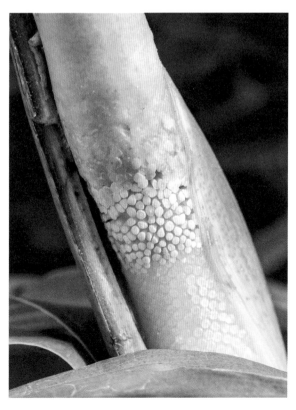

them on my pants, but I'm an animal, so don't be like me. Each berry usually bears one to three seeds. Occasionally you'll find no seeds inside the berries, or only unformed, clear seeds. This happens more often with hybrids than species, but it can be very discouraging. The good news is that you can often find at least a few good seeds in the batch.

For both anthuriums and other aroid seeds, I've found that the easiest way to gather seeds from a large quantity of fruit is to seal the fruit in a zip lock bag and then gently mash the contents into pulp with my fingers. Then I add a few inches of water to the bag, so that the seeds sink to the bottom of the bag while most of the pulp floats. Then I pour out the pulpy water. I do this repeatedly until the seeds inside the bag are clean enough to plant. Some growers treat the extracted seeds with a mild fungicide, and this may help with better germination rates and viable seedlings, but I have had success without using fungicides.

One of the most important things to know about growing aroids from seed is that the seeds need to be planted almost immediately after harvesting. They cannot easily be stored and they quickly lose viability as they age. And never let them dry out. I have heard of growers storing them in clean water and changing the water every day or so, but I haven't done this myself to test it.

Planting Seeds

Once the seeds are clean, prepare sterile AAA New Zealand sphagnum moss (available from online orchid supply companies or eBay) or very well-draining potting mix with lots of chunks of horticultural charcoal and orchid bark (see the mix on page 168). A well-draining potting mix is very important so that your seeds don't mold or rot. I use seventy-two plug flats for planting, but you can find lots of different-size trays online or at grower suppliers.

Premoisten the surface of the growing media before lightly pressing one clean seed onto the surface of each cell of your chosen growing medium. Do not bury them. Place one seed in each cell of the tray. I find they grow better this way—there is no competition and you have fewer fungal issues if everyone has their own space. You can also toss them all in one communal pot, but that's the lazy man's way and you'll have more damping off from fungus and lack of air circulation from the close quarters. You may lose some seedlings.

Keep them in a warm, humid location (around 70°F and 80 percent humidity is best). If you're concerned that your humidity is too low, cover the trays with a plastic lid. This also helps to deter snails, which absolutely love baby aroids. (Apparently, the more rare the seeds, the more irresistible they are to snails.)

You'll see small seedling sprouts in the first week. I've noticed that their growth rate depends on the size of the seed I start with. The seeds of some anthurium species (such as *A. wendlingeri*) are the size of grains of sand, while others

(such as *A. clarinervium*) may be the size of small corn kernels—larger seeds store more food for the growing anthurium, so they generally grow much more rapidly.

After the seedlings grow a leaf or two, carefully transplant them into 4-inch pots or small hanging baskets. Generally, the first new leaf of aroid seedlings is heart-shaped, no matter what its eventual shape will be.

Vegetative Propagation

If you decide that seed propagation is too time consuming, you may prefer vegetative propagation, in which you take cuttings (trim off pieces) from a plant and then root the cuttings to create new plants, or clones, of the parent plant. One important caveat: always start with a healthy plant. Sick or weak plants should not be used for cuttings. The last thing an ailing mother plant needs is to lose its growing tip. An exception, of course, is if you think the plant will die and hope to preserve a clone by quickly propagating a piece of it.

Timing is important with vegetative propagation—spring and summer are the best time to do it. I never propagate during the winter, even though I have more free time then. (Okay, I used to do it in winter, but after many failures, I finally learned my lesson.) I usually don't make cuttings after October, simply because as the days grow shorter, success becomes more elusive. Even if it's still warm out, your plants know the days are short, and you can lose both the cutting and the mother plant by overzealous cutting at the wrong time of year. I normally start cuttings on March 1. With more delicate or valuable plants, I wait a bit longer to take cuttings. By June, I can cut anything, and even if I throw the cutting in the bushes, it will still root quicker than a March cutting will.

TAKING A TIP CUTTING

Many aroids can be propagated by rooting tip cuttings. A tip cutting is a piece of the plant cut from the top of the plant or the top of a stem that has a growth point (the point where new leaves emerge). Before you start cutting a plant, however, ensure that the stem you want to cut is mature and substantial enough to avoid rotting in the planting media, which can happen when cuttings are taken from soft, new growth. You should also ensure that you leave enough of the mother plant intact so that it has sufficient energy to continue to grow. The best way to determine how much stem to leave on the mother plant is to take less than 50 percent of the plant for tip or stem (see page 155) cuttings, which means that 50 percent of the mother plant will remain intact. Taking too many cuttings from a mother plant can weaken or even kill the plant.

Make a clean cut just below the second or third node (the point of leaf attachment) from the tip of the stem. You can dust any node or nodes that will be below the soil level with rooting hormone to speed along the rooting process. (I do this especially if I'm propagating off season, which of course I never do.)

Plant the cutting in its own pot vertically, cut end down, carefully tucking it into the planting medium below the first or second node. You should have at least one node above the planting medium. Remove any leaves that will be below the medium. New Zealand AAA sphagnum moss or a loose, well-draining planting mix works best for rooting cuttings, but I find the healthiest roots are formed in sphagnum moss. The most important factor is that the media be well-draining; you don't want your little cutting to rot in oversaturated soil before it starts to root. Then water it thoroughly. You shouldn't have to water it again for a week or so, and because it has no roots, its water use will be minimal at first.

Place the potted cutting in a bright (but not full sun) spot that's a bit brighter than you would normally use for tropical plants; a little extra light seems to help cuttings grow roots. Healthy cuttings will root within four to six weeks. The cuttings also need ample humidity (70 to 80 percent), which helps keep the leaves from losing moisture and drying out and encourages healthy root growth. If your cuttings are in a greenhouse and you have a mister on a timer, placing your root cuttings under the mister can encourage them to root more quickly. If you are growing indoors and misting isn't practical, you can cover the planted cuttings to retain humidity in a few different ways:

→ Use humidity domes or cloches to cover the seedlings. These are available online or at growers' supply companies.

→ Make tents with plastic bags to cover, but not touch, the new cuttings. Add several bamboo stakes around the edges of each pot to support the plastic bag and create a little greenhouse space.

→ Cut the bottom from a clear, plastic 2-liter soda bottle and place the bottle over the cutting like a cloche. If you leave the cap on, you'll get great humidity, but the bottle will fog up and it will be difficult to see your beautiful plant. I like to leave the cap off.

→ Make mini terrariums for your cuttings using two 32-ounce clear plastic cups. Add drainage holes to the bottom cup before adding planting media. After watering the cutting, place the second cup on top like a dome.

→ Use a clear plastic bin with a lid. Fill the bottom of the bin with 2 or 3 inches of hydroton clay pebbles (aka lightweight expanded clay aggregate, or LECA). Top with a couple inches of moistened perlite, and fill the bin with an inch or so of water. Plant your cuttings directly in the perlite and cover them with the lid. (This system also works wonderfully for new imports or for any plant that needs to be reestablished. Make sure, however, that there are no pests or disease present on the plant material before you add the lid. You don't want to host a little pest commune in your warm, humid, enclosed propagation bin.)

TAKING A STEM CUTTING

After you take a tip cutting, your mother plant may still have quite a bit of stem left. As long as you leave enough stem material (at least 50 percent of the plant) on the mother plant so that it can produce enough energy to help it regrow, you can take stem cuttings at the same time as you take the tip cutting. You can then propagate small sections of stem from the mother plant. The best time to do this is in the spring or summer when the light is best. This isn't something to attempt in the winter unless you're growing indoors under artificial lights that are timed to reflect the lighting in a normal growing season.

Many of my plants are so huge by the time I propagate in the spring that a tip cutting won't fit in a 4-inch pot. So I cut a section of stem into several pieces, each at

least 2 inches long, making sure there are at least two nodes on each cutting. I place each cutting lying on its side on top of the growing media in its own 6-inch pot.

As with tip cuttings, stem cuttings require additional humidity to set roots. See the preceding section, "Taking a Tip Cutting" (page 151), for several ideas for covering cuttings to ensure that they retain humidity.

After a few weeks, the once dormant nodes will start to grow into new stems. Once a node stem reaches a decent size, 6 inches or so, and has its own roots, you can either plant the entire stem and the new plant together, or very carefully cut each new shoot, including its roots, off the stem and plant each rooted shoot.

I occasionally propagate creeping philodendrons such as *P. gloriosum* or *P. lynamii* by slicing through a horizontal stem or rhizome and leaving the cutting intact, in the pot. After a few weeks, the cutting will send up a growth point from the severed piece. Once it starts to grow and make its own leaves and roots, you can separate the new plantlet (as discussed in "Making Divisions" on page 162).

WATER PROPAGATION

Rooting your cuttings in water is an easy way to create more plants to expand your collection or share with your friends. Water propagation is a viable option for rooting cuttings from many aroids, especially philodendrons and monsteras.

About a quarter inch below a node with a leaf attached, make a clean cut to create a 6- to 8-inch cutting. Then place about a third of the cutting, cut side down, into water, removing any leaves that fall below the waterline. You can also add a tiny bit of liquid fertilizer and rooting hormone to the water to help speed things along. I usually change the water every week or so to keep it fresh.

If you have an aquarium bubbler, you can use it to oxygenate the water, which greatly speeds up the rooting process. You'll need to use a larger container such as a mason jar. Place the tube with the air stone in the water, plug in the aquarium pump, and you're ready to go.

Some plants will start to form roots almost immediately, while others seem to take forever—just as you're about to give up hope, you'll see some growth. It usually takes a few weeks for root formation to begin. After several 2- or 3-inch-long roots form, you can transfer the little plant to its permanent home in a pot. Keep in mind that the roots formed from water culture are completely different from and much more delicate than the roots your cutting would grow if it were in soil, so place the plant carefully in the potting media to avoid breaking the fragile roots. (See page 178 for potting instructions.)

Air layering is a simple propagation method that enables you to create a new plant without actually cutting and removing a piece of the mother plant—the new plant grows roots while still attached to the mother plant. This type of propagation is appropriate for some of the delicate varieties that may be a little difficult to propagate otherwise, such as *Anthurium warocqueanum*. Air layering requires a moist environment for roots to form, and this is provided by moistened sphagnum moss.

First, soak a handful of AAA New Zealand sphagnum moss in a container of water for at least an hour, until the moss is completely rehydrated. Using warm water can speed up this process. Wring out any excess water, and then wrap the damp moss around the stem of the mother plant, around the bottom node.

The moss should extend a few inches above and below the bottom node. You can remove the bottom leaf if necessary. Most aroids will have some aerial roots already starting to grow; this will greatly speed up your propagation. Completely cover the damp moss with plastic, such as food wrap, and use plant twine to secure the plastic-wrapped moss around the plant stem. The wrapped moss will retain moisture and encourage root growth. You can slice a few small holes in the plastic to help avoid rot. After two to four weeks, roots will extend into the moss from the node. You can then cut off the stem below the newly formed roots and repot the rooted cutting. The stem remaining on the plant will eventually send out a new growth point, usually from the side or bottom of the stem.

PROPAGATION BY STOLONS OR RUNNERS

Stolons, aka runners, are slender stems that grow horizontally from a mother plant and along the top of the soil (see photo, opposite, of stolon growing out of the pot and onto the pedestal). Stolons send out intermittent roots that attach to soil, where they absorb nutrients and water to feed new plantlets. I've had *Monstera obliqua* runners crawling all over my greenhouse benches, searching for some magical perfect situation in which to send out roots for a new plant. They may run across ten pots before deciding they like the eleventh, and that's where they put down roots and start growing a new plant.

Some growers cut off the runners and propagate growth nodes straight into another pot, before they root. This works, but I get healthier plants and faster growth if I leave the runners attached to the mother plant for awhile. The mother is already rooted and passes nutrients on to the young plant to give it a head start. If you sever the runners before they grow their own root systems or leaves, they will eventually grow, but it will take them longer to get established and start growing. I usually set the pot of the plant that I want to propagate onto a tray of sphagnum moss, and when the plant's runners touch the moss, they generally get right to the important business of getting comfortable and forming little plantlets and roots. Once the roots and plantlets form, you can cut the runner and pot the babies up into their own pots.

If you have purchased runners or want to root runners severed from the mother plant, the easiest place to grow them is in clear plastic storage bins in moist sphagnum moss. First, place expanded clay balls, aka LECA balls, about 2 or 3 inches deep in the bottom of the container. The clay balls give the excess water a place to drain so that the sphagnum moss doesn't stay too wet and rot. Next, you'll need to moisten enough moss to cover the LECA balls with a layer about 3 to 4 inches thick. Soak the moss in a large bowl or bucket of warm water for at least an hour until the moss has sufficiently soaked up all the water it can. Then use your hands to wring it out as much as possible. (I find it's easier to do this in small batches, and over a sink.) After you have squeezed out excess water, use your fingers to loosen up the moss and spread it evenly on top of the LECA balls.

To speed up the growing process a bit, you can use orchid cloning paste, which includes natural plant hormones (cytokinins) to trick the plant into cloning itself. (Note that plant cytokinins, which stimulate node and plant growth, are different from auxins, which stimulate root growth.) Use a cotton swab to transfer the cloning paste onto the runner's nodes, and then place the runner into the moss. You should start to see some activation and buds forming within two to three weeks. By the time a plantlet has formed two or three leaves, it should also have a decent root system, and you can plant it in its own pot.

MAKING DIVISIONS

Some plants will send up pups (side shoots or offsets growing from the base of the mother plant) that you can separate from the mother to create new plants. The best way to divide a new pup from the mother plant is very carefully! Although dividing plants is messy business, I prefer not to wear gloves so I can feel the roots and the attached pups.

First, take the plant out of the pot and gently brush some of the soil off the roots with your fingers to see how the pups are connected. Sometimes a pup curves under the roots of the mother plant, and sometimes it's attached at the base of the mother plant. Gently start to work the pup and its roots loose from the mother plant. You may have to unwind some of the mother plant's roots. Use clippers to carefully cut the roots apart, making sure that the mother and pup each end up with plenty of roots of their own. Once an offset is separated, use a dusting of rooting hormone on its roots to give it a head start. Carefully pot up the pup in its own pot, and then repot the mother plant and clean up your mess.

CHAPTER SIX

Caring for Extraordinary Plants

I don't think you can become an accomplished grower until you kill a few plants. (With that criteria, I am a wonderful grower.) I don't mean kill them on purpose, of course, but after numerous attempts at growing and failing, you learn what works and what doesn't work, and this eventually evolves into knowledge of proper plant care. There is no single perfect way to grow plants, because we are all working in different conditions. Growers use many different growing media, fertilizers, and watering schedules—we all have to determine what works best for us.

Some of the best advice in the world comes from friends and books. Once, a friend who was a nursery owner came to visit and told me that I grow my plants too wet. Well, maybe I do, but I also grow them in very small pots in a very loose soil mix, and this works for me. Plus, it never stops raining in South Florida in the summer—I can't turn it off. If I took a plant from another nursery that was planted in heavier soil and planted it in a large pot here in my wet world, it would surely rot.

Despite the best (or worst) advice, you'll eventually learn what does and doesn't work so that you can begin to adjust your care routine. Almost everything I have learned about plant care came from the mistakes I made, and we all make growing mistakes. The trick is to make less of them as we learn more about our chosen plant family. Never be afraid to ask for advice about how to grow your new plants. All kinds of social media groups specialize in rare plants, and folks are more than happy to offer help. So many people have been exactly where you are. It's easy to think that everyone knows what they're doing when all you see are perfect plant images online. But keep in mind that most people don't post pictures of brown leaves and dead plants on Instagram or Facebook. I know I don't.

Watering

To set up a watering schedule, start by observing your plants. It's doubtful that they'll all need water at the same time: some dry out faster and some like the soil a bit wetter in general. Anthuriums, for example, prefer to be in soil that's on the dry side rather than too wet. I suggest you check your new plants every two days until you get to know their watering needs.

Before you water, stick your finger down into the soil a couple inches; soil can appear dry on the surface but be sopping wet in the middle of the pot. Obviously, if the soil is still wet from the last watering, it doesn't need more water. If you don't want to ruin your perfectly manicured nails, you can find a good moisture meter at a plant nursery, garden center, or online. Just stick the probe into the soil about 80 percent of the way down into the pot. Wait about sixty seconds for your reading. On a meter with a dial display, a midrange moisture reading is what you're after. On a digital meter, the best range is 15 to 17 percent moisture.

Overwatering is the best way to encourage rot and kill potted plants. It's difficult for a plant to bounce back from rot. On the other hand, no tropical plant likes to dry out completely between waterings, unlike many other houseplants. If roots completely dry out and dehydrate, they can become brittle and damaged, and this damage is permanent—they lose the ability to take up water and the plant will die.

As you become more experienced, you'll be able to notice the clues from your plants when they're thirsty. Wilting, curling leaves, and hanging leaf stalks, for example, indicate that your plants could use a drink. After a while, you'll realize which plants need water every few days and which ones can wait as long as two weeks.

Plants use more water in the warmer months during the growing season, when they are actively putting on new leaves, and you'll need to adjust your watering schedule accordingly. Plants in brighter light or those growing outdoors will also grow much faster (the extra sunlight provides more energy), so a plant in brighter light may need more water than the same plant in a darker location, because it will convert the brighter light to energy and will grow larger.

You don't need special equipment to water indoor plants, but you can probably find an excuse to get yourself a top-of-the-line long-spouted watering can for all those hard-to-reach plants. It may be easier to take smaller plants to the sink for watering and let them drain completely there. It is always important to water thoroughly so that the water drains all the way through the pot and all the roots receive moisture, not just those on the surface. It's better to water deeply—until water is draining out the bottom of the pot—less frequently than to water plants shallowly more often.

You can alternatively set a pot in a very shallow (half inch) dish of water. It will be wicked into the pot through the drainage hole. This will keep water off the leaves. It might strike you as odd, but when growing indoors, it's a bad idea to get tropical plant leaves wet. How could it be bad to wet the leaves when these plants originated in a rainforest? The answer is simple: When the plants are outdoors, air circulation keeps disease and fungus from getting established. Indoor plants aren't so lucky.

Next, consider using bottled or filtered water if you aren't sure about the quality of your tap water. Some cities add a lot of chlorine to the water, and other water systems contain tons of minerals—some good, some not so good. It's easy to have your water tested if you think quality may be an issue. I recall Dewey Fisk using the most awful iron-laden swamp water for his plants. Everything was stained brown from the rust—as a matter of fact, I still have stained plant labels from him that show their years of service. The plants didn't seem to suffer from this, but the pots still looked rough from the staining.

If you can collect rainwater for your plants, they will appreciate the effort. Rainwater is the gold standard as far as plants are concerned. I've noticed I can water all I want, but as soon as the summer rains come, the plants really start growing lush new leaves. I've been meaning to get a reverse osmosis water system, because this is about the closest you can come to rainwater.

Wilted Leaves

Wilted leaves aren't always a sign that a plant needs water; in fact, sometimes it's quite the opposite. Wilting can indicate rotted roots that can no longer take up water properly. I often see plants posted for sale online that obviously have poor roots—their leaves have a dull look and hang just a little bit—sure signs that the roots are in poor shape.

Creating the Right Soil Mix

When you're growing aroids, it's important to address soil drainage and nutrients. Aroids are heavy feeders during the growing season and they insist on proper drainage. It is very important that anthuriums, in particular, are planted in a well-draining soil mix. As with many aroids, they like lots of water, but they certainly don't want to sit wet.

More people have killed their plants by overwatering than anything else, but the term *overwatering* is misleading. If the soil is draining properly, it is very difficult to overwater. In their natural rainforest homes, most aroids would be constantly wet, but they aren't growing in mud. Their normal growing media is mostly leaf litter, bits of tree bark, and detritus that fell from the plants and trees above them.

There really is no one-size-fits-all potting media, but you can create a mix that is somewhat similar to natural growing conditions with the right ingredients. In general, a good mix that includes orchid bark and horticultural charcoal can really help keep the soil loose and aerated and can keep plants' roots healthy. If you're growing several different kinds of plants, you may need to make slightly different mixes depending on each plant's needs. If you make your own soil mix, you can add whatever you like to accommodate each plant. Growing conditions are different for everyone, and we all need to use what works best for our particular plants.

Several ingredients are important additives in a good growing mix to produce a loose, well-draining blend that mimics aroids' natural growing media:

Orchid bark Aroid roots love to attach to damp pieces of orchid bark to absorb the moisture they contain. Like perlite, orchid bark also prevents the soil from becoming too compacted by creating air spaces between soil particles.

Horticultural charcoal The carbon in charcoal traps soil odors and impurities, and it helps prevent mold. As an old grower once told me, "It keeps the roots sweet."

Perlite This volcanic glass product is used in soil mixes to help aerate the soil. The white granules create air space in the soil and improve drainage to help the soil resist compaction. Many commercially sold planting mixes include perlite.

Vermiculite This natural mineral is used in many soil mixes to improve aeration and absorb nutrients. It also retains water very well, which helps speed up seed germination.

Pumice Pumice is a highly porous lava rock that is great for proper drainage. It also aerates heavy soil and helps the plant create a healthier root system.

Organic
potting soil

Orchid bark

Perlite

Horticultural
charcoal

You can purchase ready-made planting mixes, but, even better, you can mix your own general-purpose mix for indoor tropical plants and adjust that to suit particular plants. My mix includes about 40 percent organic potting soil, 25 percent orchid bark, 25 percent horticultural charcoal, and 10 percent perlite. If you need soil with better drainage for a particularly fussy plant, you can add a little vermiculite and pumice.

Fertilizing

I usually add some time-released fertilizer (I like Nutricote) to the growing media and mix it all in before I repot a plant. I think this is better than piling all the fertilizer on top of the soil—the roots get an even distribution of fertilizer rather than a few hot spots where the fertilizer is concentrated. For the correct quantity of fertilizer, follow the directions on the bag, since the amount of fertilizer you'll use depends on the size of your pot.

I prefer to think of fertilizer as plant vitamins rather than plant food. Fertilizer should never be used as a substitute for quality soil, just as vitamins are not a good substitute for a healthy diet. Also, you should never rush to fertilize a struggling plant. If it already has a weakened root system or disease, adding a bunch of fertilizer can just add to the plant's stress and may finish it off.

After a while, potting soil will degrade as the plant absorbs vitamins and minerals and they leach out in the water that runs out of the pot. Fertilizer is important because it helps restore some of the lost macronutrients that potted plants need to grow strong and healthy.

I use Nutricote 18-6-8 time-released fertilizer. Whether they are planted indoors and outdoors, plants take up much more fertilizer during the growing season. I find using less fertilizer more often is better than forgetting to fertilize and then dumping a fistful in all at once. Overfertilizing can burn your plants and cause a buildup of plant-damaging salts.

I also use Maxsea, a great seaweed-based fertilizer that includes lots of trace minerals and secondary nutrients (calcium, magnesium, and sulfur). It's also great for greening up chlorotic (yellowing) leaves. I consider it to be more of a plant

NPK

When you are researching fertilizers, you'll notice that each package features three numbers that represent the percentages of nitrogen (chemical symbol N), phosphorus (P), and potassium (K) in the mix (NPK for short), in that order. Fertilizers with a high nitrogen content (such as 18-6-8) are best during the growing season for encouraging green growth. If you want to stimulate healthy roots and flowers, look for a fertilizer with higher amounts of phosphorus and potassium, such as 15-30-15.

food that supports the health of my plants long term rather than just providing a quick boost.

You can give your plant a quick boost by foliar feeding using a weak liquid fertilizer spray. This does wonders to perk up a neglected plant, and it helps produce stronger plants and stimulates growth. Seaweed fertilizers, in particular, are great for this, but you can use any of the organic liquid fertilizers. Mix the fertilizer with water about a quarter strength of what the package directions say and spray it directly on the leaves. If you are an indoor grower, you can avoid making a mess by spraying your plant over the sink or in the bath or shower. Let the leaves dry before moving the plant back to its spot.

SYNTHETIC VS. ORGANIC FERTILIZERS

A word about synthetic fertilizers: They may give plants a quick nutrient boost, but they may not include many of the micronutrients that plants need in the long term. They can also be dangerous to plants if they're overused or mixed too strongly. Fertilizer burn is no fun. The plant's leaves, particularly their edges and tips, will turn brown and look burnt. If you accidentally use too much fertilizer, don't despair. Remove the plant from the pot and wash off the soil around its roots. Carefully. Then repot the plant in fresh soil. Check on it every few days to see how it's doing. A synthetic fertilizer like Nutricote is great for a quick jolt and to green-up plants quickly, but if it were something for people, it would be like drinking a double espresso instead of taking care of yourself and eating right!

Organic fertilizers, on the other hand, release nutrients more slowly and evenly. They're made from natural living sources, such as fish emulsion, seaweed, and blood and bone meal. They also contain trace minerals and nutrients that plants need to thrive. Naturally occurring microbes and fungi break down the nutrients in organic fertilizers, which are quickly taken up by a plant's roots. Organic fertilizers are much safer than synthetic versions, and it is more difficult to overdose plants by using too much. Seaweed-based fertilizers (such as Maxsea) are wonderful sources of nutrients that are readily available to growing plants.

Fertilizer Burn

One of my most spectacular fertilizer mistakes was using Osmocote outdoors in South Florida. The supplier insisted that it contained the same components used in the Nutricote I was accustomed to using. The nitrogen in the fertilizer is released more rapidly in hot weather. I certainly wouldn't recommend it for use in small pots in outdoor conditions. You may be able to get away with using it indoors where the climate isn't as harsh and the fertilizer won't be released as quickly. When I used it on several plants in my greenhouse one afternoon, every poor little plant fried, including an entire crop of baby *Anthurium wendlingeri* plants. And I had to wait seven years for my *A. wendlingeri* to set seed again.

You can also add a bit of compost or manure to your plants, but if you are growing indoors, this might be a little too "earthy" for your senses. Many of the organic fertilizers may also produce a strong smell, especially when they're used indoors, so be sure to check for this before using a stinky product to fertilize every plant in your house. When you use organic fertilizers, you may not see immediate results, but give them time to work. They really are the best way to promote the overall health of your plants.

MACRONUTRIENTS AND MICRONUTRIENTS

In simple terms, plants need macronutrients in relatively large quantities, and micronutrients are needed in relatively small quantities. Both are essential to the health of your plants. Your soil and fertilizer should supply the following macronutrients: nitrogen, phosphorus, potassium, magnesium, sulfur, and calcium. It should include the following micronutrients: boron, iron, manganese, copper, cobalt, zinc, chlorine, and molybdenum.

Choosing the Right Container

You can use any container for your plant, as long as it has drainage holes. Plastic and glazed ceramic pots maintain soil moisture better than unglazed pots (such as terra cotta), but this can be a negative if you are heavy handed with the watering. The soil in unglazed clay pots can dry out pretty quickly because these pots are porous, so water can seep through. It's a good idea to use either a glazed or plastic saucer to catch water that drains from the pot rather than a clay saucer for the same reason.

Nursery containers are generally made of cheap plastic and aren't usually attractive, but they can be set inside decorative pots. You can change pots easily this way without having to repot your plants, and because the plastic is flexible, they are easier to remove when you are ready to repot. You can also reuse nursery pots, give them to nurseries to reuse, or recycle some of them. (Not all types are recyclable, so check with your local recycling center.) They are quite lightweight, and although this is great if you have to take plants to the sink to water, it can make a plant more unstable as it gets larger and more top-heavy.

The Importance of Drainage

I can't overstress the importance of drainage. Without proper drainage, aroids are extremely prone to rot. If you want to use a decorative pot that has no drainage holes, pot up your plant in a container with holes (or use the nursery pot) and then set the entire plant and container into the decorative pot. If the container sits too low in the pot, add an inch or two of gravel in the bottom of the pot and set the container on top of the gravel.

The sky's the limit when using decorative glazed pots, with many different styles and colors to choose from that go with any décor. Although they are probably the most expensive pots, they can last forever, are reusable, and are simple to clean to prepare for new plants. They also can be heavy, and although this adds to the stability of your plants and makes it more difficult for your pets to knock them over, it also makes them difficult to move. If you do need to move a ceramic pot, take care not to set the pot down too hard because it can easily crack or break.

Growing Climbing Anthuriums on Totems and in Baskets

Climbing anthurium plants will ramble around, with their extremely long, stretched internodes (distances between leaves) looking for something to climb on. Without providing support for these climbers, they will sometimes snap from the weight of their large and abundant foliage. You can use a totem for vertical support or plant an anthurium in a hanging basket, where its long leaves can hang downward.

USING A TOTEM FOR SUPPORT

Anthuriums, especially some of the larger leaved varieties, require a sturdy climbing support, and a totem is a beautiful way to display a climbing plant. In their natural environment, these rainforest plants climb up trees or any other vertical structure or plant to reach higher up into the rainforest canopy to access more light, and they send out aerial roots as anchors.

A vertical totem provides a place for climbing plants to grasp and grow vertically in your home, and it encourages them to grow larger leaves. Totems for home use can be made of tree fern, wood, or poles wrapped in sphagnum moss or coir. They are often available at plant nurseries or online.

When placing a totem, it's important that you push the bottom of the totem as far down as possible into the soil for added stability. You can gently tie your plant to the totem to help it make its way skyward, and keep the totem lightly misted so the roots of your plant will attach to it.

GROWING ANTHURIUMS IN A HANGING BASKET

Epiphytic anthuriums usually grow in trees or on the sides of cliffs. They also require proper air circulation and drainage. To accommodate their needs, I plant them in wooden baskets with sphagnum moss packed around their stems and aerial roots. This gives them room for the leaves to grow downward while offering proper drainage. The roots will attach to the wood and hang over the sides of the basket. Many plants grow well this way, but I find it a pain to repot them. If the roots are attached to the wood, I usually repot the whole basket into a new one to avoid disturbing them.

Leaf Morph in Aroids

An unusual thing about many climbing aroids is the absolutely amazing difference between an immature plant and a mature climbing plant. When I started collecting aroids, it once occurred to me that I had been repeatedly buying the same philodendron in different stages of maturity! The leaves of some shingling aroids, such as *Monstera dubia*, change completely between their juvenile and mature states (see photo, above). This is probably an energy saving mechanism for the plant: When searching for a suitable climbing host, plants produce small leaves and ramble around until they find something to climb. Only when they find something sturdy to climb will they begin to grow mature leaves. Most aroids with fenestrated leaves don't develop them until they climb and mature a bit.

Repotting

Repotting refers to moving a plant from one pot to a different pot. There are many reasons to repot a plant. Perhaps you bought a new decorative pot, or your grandmother gave you an old pot that she loved. Or maybe the plant has grown too large for its pot. The term *potting up* refers to installing a plant into a larger pot as it grows.

Your plants can often tell you when it's time to repot. Its roots may pop out of the pot's drainage holes. Sometimes plants push themselves up and out of a pot a bit as the roots wind around the inside of the pot. If a plant always seems to be dry, even soon after watering it, this could mean that there are more roots in the pot than water-retaining soil, and the water is running right through the pot.

The best time of year to repot your plants is in the spring or summer while they are actively in growth, which helps them recover faster. I've noticed more active plant growth after I repot—as if the plant were just waiting for the extra space to stretch out. I recommend repotting houseplants once or twice a year, especially if you use tap water to water them. Most tap water contains chlorine and other chemicals that can build up in the pot's soil and damage your plants. If you use a water softener, excess salt in the water can build up in the soil and slowly kill your plants. If you suspect that chemicals have built up in the soil, before you repot the plant, carefully remove most of the soil from around its roots and plant the pot in clean soil.

When your plants are ready to be potted up into a larger pot, use the next largest size pot, perhaps one that's an inch or two wider and taller. It's easy to overwater a plant when there is so much extra soil in the pot.

If you're repotting indoors, first put down some plastic sheeting or some repurposed cardboard as a surface protector—you don't want to ruin your rugs or furniture. This also helps keep soil and fertilizer from spreading everywhere and is a huge help at cleanup time.

If you're repotting from a plastic pot, tip the plant on its side, tap the bottom of the pot, and gently squeeze the sides all the way around to loosen the soil and roots. You can usually remove the old pot without harming the plant. If it

Reusing Pots and Soil

Don't reuse a pot that a previous plant has died in without sanitizing it first, because fungus, bacteria, or pests (or whatever killed the plant) may be lurking in the old pot. To sanitize a pot, soak it in a solution of one part bleach to nine parts water for about fifteen minutes. Then wash the pot with dish soap, rinse it well, and let it air dry. As tempting as it can be to reuse old soil, it's best to dump it outside in your compost pile rather than risk contaminating your newly potted plants.

doesn't come off easily because the roots have attached to the pot or your plant is extremely root bound, carefully cut down the sides of the pot and peel it off the plant roots like a jacket.

If you're repotting from a ceramic or clay pot, carefully tip the plant on its side, tap the bottom of the pot, and push a butter knife along the edge of the pot and run it around the side to loosen the soil. If the plant doesn't want to come out of the pot, you may have to break the pot off the plant by gently tapping it with a hammer. I say *gently*, because if you are too aggressive, the sharp pot shards may fly everywhere. (For this reason, you might wear eye protection.)

Gently remove the plant from the pot and check its roots, being careful not to break or damage them. Roots are covered in tiny, delicate root hairs, which absorb nutrients and water. If you snap off roots, you are inviting bacteria and fungus that can harm your plant. Think of it as an open wound.

If most of the soil falls away, you probably don't need to repot. Do your best to replace the plant and soil, carefully, into the original pot. But if the whole plant and root ball pop out in the shape of the pot and the roots are tightly wound, it's definitely time to repot. If the roots are tightly wound, carefully unwind and loosen them before you replant—again, taking care not to break the roots. Carefully place your plant in the new pot. You may need to add a little soil in the bottom of the pot to raise the plant to the same level it was planted before. Most plants, especially aroids, do not want to be potted too deeply and do not like to be buried in soil that covers the base of any petioles (leaf stalks). And for philodendrons and anthuriums with creeping rhizomes, the rhizome should remain above the soil level.

Gently add more potting mix around the plant's roots, tamping and carefully shaking the soil in place. Use your fingers, a bamboo stake, or a chopstick to pack the soil carefully into any air pockets, being sure not to press too firmly—you can damage the roots if you compact the soil too much. Once your plant is all tucked into its new pot, it's time to water it in. Give it a good, even soaking and let it drain.

Grooming and Observing Your Plants

If you're growing indoors, it's a good idea to check your plants occasionally for issues other than just moisture levels. Grooming plants involves more than just occasionally watering and fertilizing. Here are a few tips for plant caretaking.

If plants are facing natural light from a window, rotate your plant every month or two to ensure even growth. If you don't rotate your plant periodically, you'll notice most of the plant's growth will be directed toward the source of light.

To clean away any dust or buildup from the leaves, wipe them down occasionally with a clean cloth and watered-down dish soap (use about a tablespoon of dish soap per quart of water). This is also a good time to check the plants for pests.

There are different schools of thought about whether you should cut old, dying, or diseased leaves off your plant or let them remain. I cannot stand to see

damaged leaves on my plants and usually pinch them off. Some people believe that because damaged leaves are still making food for the plant through photosynthesis, they should be left attached. Others, like me, think that if a leaf is diseased or has insect damage, it's important to remove it so that the disease doesn't spread or in case insects or eggs remain on the leaf so that they don't spread to the rest of the plant.

The trick is not to overgroom—touching, squeezing, and rubbing the leaves and removing the plant from the pot to check the roots too often. I have loved a lot of plants to death this way. (My first ae-ae banana plant was a gorgeous, variegated plant with white splotches of color on the leaves. I potted it up and then decided it needed a bigger pot. Then I added some fertilizer someone recommended, but I didn't like it, so I repotted it again. It eventually gave up on me. I mourned.)

Walk around and observe your plants regularly to get to know your growing conditions and your plants. Observation is a vitally important skill when you're growing plants. Learn to read your plants so you know when they need more water, light, or fertilizer, or when they have pests or diseases. One of my favorite things to do with my plants (other than propagating and making more plants) is to meander around the shade house and take pictures. I especially love new leaves. (By the way, if you've never met a new, rolled up *Anthurium veitchii* leaf, you haven't truly lived. It's amazing. When a young leaf emerges, it just a few inches long, but over a period of a couple weeks the leaf grows until it maxes out at 3 feet long.) Observing my plants regularly helps me determine which plants need repotting, spraying, or petting, and I often rediscover plants that I'd forgotten about. I can't tell you how many times I've been in the shade houses lovingly taking pictures when I noticed a plant I had forgotten about hiding among the leaves of other plants.

Increasing Your Humidity

In chapter two, I explained how to check your humidity before buying plants, but even so, sometimes you may find that your plants need a little extra humidity. For example, velvet-leaved aroids seem to appreciate more shade and humidity than most bird's nest anthuriums; they need to stay more evenly moist and are very sensitive to drying out. Velvets also seem extremely sensitive to spider mites when grown hot and dry. (Mmm, tasty velvet!!)

Kitchens and bathrooms are probably the most naturally humid places in your house. Most plants appreciate the humidity in a bathroom, kitchen, or laundry room, as long as there is ample light.

Another way to improve humidity is to try grouping plants closer together. Keep an eye on crowded plant areas, however, which can create a breeding ground for pests. (See page 190 for more on pests and pest control.) You can also make a pebble tray for several plants, which is not only helpful in raising the humidity a bit, but provides some visual interest. Simply add decorative pebbles and a couple inches of water to a shallow tray. Then place a few pots of plants of assorted shapes and sizes into the tray, ensuring that each plant has adequate space. As the water in the tray evaporates, it increases the humidity around the plants. Voilà! Done! So easy!

HUMIDIFIERS

If you need even more humidity, try using a humidifier. (Elechomes and Levoit seem to be the best humidifiers for indoor plants.) Here are few tips about using humidifiers:

→ Most have a humidity setting and will automatically turn off when they reach that point. Maintain about 55 to 75 percent humidity, depending on the plants involved. Anthuriums like the higher levels (70 to 80 percent), while philodendrons and monsteras prefer 60 to 70 percent.

→ Set your humidifier on a table to create a more even humidity level.

→ Tap water and spring water include minerals, so use distilled water in your humidifier to cut down on mineral residue on your plants and inside the humidifier, which can clog the humidifier.

→ Keep the humidifier about 4 to 6 feet away from plants, and try to avoid aiming the humidifier's airflow directly at your plants. You don't want their leaves to stay wet all the time without proper air circulation.

→ Avoid aiming the humidifier's airflow directly at furniture or walls. Although there is a misconception that a humidifier will ruin your drywall and furniture, as long as you don't point the humidifier directly at furniture and walls, and the space has good air circulation, this will not be a problem.

GROWING PLANTS IN A TERRARIUM

I have "a few" terrariums—twenty-five to be exact (the photo opposite is of one of mine). The plants love the added humidity that the terrariums provide, and I also keep captive-bred dart frogs, which appreciate the plants I grow for them in their terrariums. (I think the plants have mixed feelings about the frogs.)

IKEA MILSBO Cabinet Terrariums

Terrariums made from IKEA MILSBO glass-door cabinets are popping up a lot on social media. These metal cabinets with glass doors are commonly used in home dining and living rooms, but they can be turned into giant terrariums that can house quite a few plants. I would have them all over my house if I had the space. An IKEA Greenhouse Club Facebook group includes lots of inspirational ideas and photos showing how others are setting up their MILSBO terrariums. Check it out!

Terrarium Frogs

You can include a frog or frogs in a terrarium, but you need to add a good layer of leaf litter to provide shelter and hiding places for them. Be sure that any plants you add haven't been sprayed with chemicals and that they are pest free to avoid harming your frogs. Spiders can be a huge problem; they can be attracted by a frog's meal of fruit flies, but they may prefer to attack a nice, juicy, little frog instead. Check out www.dendroboard.com to learn more about keeping frogs.

Terrariums are a wonderful option that supply plants with some of the best growing conditions imaginable—lots of humidity, controlled air movement, and full-spectrum LED lighting. Combine all of these attributes within a terrarium to create an amazing ecosystem within your home for an incredible array of tropical plants. You can place the plants directly into a terrarium in substrate or planting media or place the plants in their original nursery pots into the terrarium. I prefer direct planting, because I want everything I do to look as natural as possible—like it just happened naturally, except inside a glass box. I like to use Exo Terra terrariums or custom terrariums with doors that open from the front, which makes it easier to install and maintain the plants.

If you want to include something for plants to climb, virgin cork bark pieces used for orchids work well. Spread silicone adhesive on the bottom of the terrarium where you want to place the bark pieces to tack them to the glass. After 24 hours or so, use Great Stuff brand spray foam sealant to affix the cork bark to the back of the terrarium and fill in any spaces between the pieces of cork bark. After another 24 hours or so, slice off any excess foam with a knife. Then cover any foam that remains by attaching bits of coir or peat moss using silicone adhesive. Don't worry if it's not perfect. Your plants will grow in fast and any mistakes will be covered.

When you're ready to add growing media and plants, start by spreading 2 or 3 inches of hydroton clay pebbles (such as LECA balls) or similar expanded clay pellets to the bottom of the terrarium to create a drainage layer. Over that, you can add substrate barrier, such as a piece of screening or landscape fabric, to keep the soil from sinking into the drainage layer; simply cut it to the correct size and place it over the hydroton pebbles. The best terrarium substrate I've used is the ABG Mix developed by the Atlanta Botanical Gardens, which you can purchase online. This mix ensures good drainage and moisture retention to keep the plant roots healthy and prevent the soil from becoming anaerobic (a situation that occurs when substrate becomes so oversaturated with water that no oxygen is present—as in a swamp).

When you're ready to add plants, carefully remove each plant from its pot and dig a small hole for each into the ABG mix with a spoon or your fingers. Place the plant in the mix and carefully tuck it in. Place taller plants and plants that will eventually be taller in the back of the terrarium to avoid blocking or crowding out the smaller plants. Cover the entire soil mix with live moss or decorative gravel. A glass terrarium top is preferred over a screen top to provide the best humidity levels. If your terrarium container doesn't come with a glass top, you can have a piece of glass cut to size to fit.

You can mist your terrarium by hand, but I prefer to use a Mist King system on a timer, which has greatly improved my success with both animals and plants. An automatic system gives the terrarium a more even and thorough misting. Look online for more information about using an automatic misting system with a terrarium.

Supplemental Lighting

In chapter two, I explained how to look at the available lighting in your home and determine the best locations for your plants, but sometimes you may notice that your plants may need a little extra light. Plants will usually turn their leaves toward the light, but if an entire plant stretches toward a light source, you can rightly assume that it needs a bit more overall light. If a plant is leaning toward the light and making smaller leaves, it definitely needs a light boost.

Tropical plants prefer about 3000 to 4000 lumens of light. Full-spectrum LED grow lights are the most efficient and effective way to increase the light to your plants. Full-spectrum lights can be used to replicate natural sunlight. Florescent lights also produce full-spectrum light, but LEDs are more energy efficient and create very little heat, which means they are better for the environment, less expensive to use, and better for your plants.

You can find some great decorative grow lights from Soltech Solutions and GE, among other manufacturers. In general, you should keep the lights about 3 feet away from foliage plants to offer them the correct amount of supplemental lighting without burning their leaves. You can use a more powerful light in the 4000 lumen range for plants that require more light than others, such as monsteras.

Controlling Temperature

You can grow your tropical houseplants outdoors during warmer months of the year if you have a porch or patio, and you'll see a huge surge in growth. Tropical plants and aroids prefer to be warm for best growth, with optimal temperatures of 70° to 85°F. Note that, in general, they will not thrive in temperatures below 70°F, and most aroids all but shut down if temperatures get below about 55°F. Commercial growers generally use 55°F as the starting temperature to begin to heat their greenhouses. They won't die at those temperatures, but they will suffer and cease growing until it warms up again. Some may even go dormant to conserve energy and wait for warmer weather. Tropical plants are more likely to die when they are stressed by cold temperatures. Prolonged cold in the 50s or prolonged heat in the 90s can be fatal.

Growing Plants in a Refrigerated Drink Cooler

This may be one of the coolest (pun intended) projects I've seen in a while, though I've yet to try it myself. A few years ago, I was visiting friend and fellow collector Mary Sizemore in Central Florida. She had set up a refrigerated drink cooler, like the kind used in a convenience store, as a terrarium for high elevation, cool temperature-loving plants. I thought this was a brilliant idea, because so many of the interesting, high-elevation Andean anthuriums and philodendrons (such as *Anthurium rugulosum* and *Anthurium cutucuense*) require reliable nighttime temperature drops of at least 10° to 20°F. I can't supply that for them naturally in South Florida, where summer temperatures hover around a 100°F, about 30°F warmer than these types of plants prefer. Temperatures in the 65° to 70°F range are usually best for these uber-finicky high-elevation plants.

These drink coolers have glass doors, which makes them easy to maintain and view the plants inside. They have exhaust fans built in, and you can create specific humidity and temperature levels inside. They also include LED lighting—but if not, you can change the lighting to something more conducive to plant growth, such as full-spectrum LED lights. And they come with shelves, which you can use as is or customize.

Hang plastic-coated wire vertically within the cooler to display mounted mini orchids and epiphytic tropical plants. Use silicone adhesive to affix virgin cork bark to the back of the cooler for climbers, which gives the plants support to attach and grow mature leaves and gives you the space to plant and use all the height that these big "terrariums" offer.

Mary is a world traveler, plant collector, and good friend, and she lives her best life doing what she loves. She is constantly trying new and exciting projects to improve her growing conditions. I want to be Mary when I grow up.

Controlling Insect Pests

I get asked all the time how I keep pests off my plants, with so many kept so close together outdoors in the shade houses. Fact is, the beneficial insects, lizards, and frogs that live in my shade houses work overtime to gobble up pests. Also, the rain washes pests off the leaves, and good air circulation helps avoid moisture situations that attract them. This is not to say I don't experience pest problems, however. I simply look for any minor issues and take care of them before they become major ones.

Carefully check your plants regularly for any little critters. Overlapping leaves provide pests with places to hide. They love to hide under leaves and down in the leaf axil where a leaf attaches to the stem. It's a simple matter to wipe the pests off leaves with a damp cloth or smash any visible bugs with a brick. (OK, wait, maybe not a brick because that's probably not good for the plants.) I generally just use my fingernail to just scrape off any bugs I find. I find it safer to spot-check plants and remove bugs manually (wo-manually?) than to use heavy pesticides. If you are checking your plants routinely for pests—and you should be—you may be able to avoid using pesticides. After all, do you really want to spray poison in your home or in any area that you or your pets may frequent?

Because I grow outdoors, I have a different group of pests and problems than indoor growers have. We have iguanas in South Florida, and the babies especially love to munch on the new growth of young anthuriums. They freeze in place when I'm around, thinking I won't see them, but they underestimate me, and I ninja-snatch them and take them for a ride to a more suitable home away from my plants. (They are lucky that they're so cute. I give them a firm talking to on the way out of my shade house. I view it as a teaching moment for them.) The other two most prevalent pests that do the most damage to my plants are snails and caterpillars—especially in the early spring when all the perfect new leaves are waking up. I can't even enjoy watching the butterflies flit around knowing they are laying eggs that hatch into rabid, marauding caterpillars.

Then, of course, there's the South Florida weather. Summer is as hot as the surface of the sun, plus we get torrential rains and hurricanes. In winter, with an occasional 45°F night and then an 85°F day, the plants don't know what the heck is going on. You would think they would get used to it. And then I have a neurotic Doberman, and I've learned never to set anything on the ground that could be used for traction when she decides to bolt after squirrels. See how lucky you are to be growing indoors?

Most of us will encounter pests that munch on our plants. Here's a list of common pests and some suggestions for how to deal with them, preferably without resorting to toxic chemicals, though a few chemical solutions are included here. With all chemical controls, make sure you follow the directions on the label, exactly. Some of them may not be recommended for indoor use or around pets.

THRIPS

These tiny, slender sucking insects feed on new leaves. Look for contorted leaves with tiny speckled areas that are sometimes silvery in color. You'll usually see the damage before you see the insects. They can transmit plant viruses as they dine on your plants.

- *NATURAL CONTROL* NEEM OIL
- *MILD CONTROL* INSECTICIDAL SOAP

FUNGUS GNATS

Adult fungus gnats are harmless, but their larvae can destroy plant roots. They are most often a problem in overwet soils. To keep their numbers down, allow the top inch or two of soil to dry out between waterings, though this won't completely keep pests at bay (and remember that aroids don't like to be completely dry between waterings, so make sure the soil below is still moist). The best treatment I have used is a product called Mosquito Bits. It contains *Bacillus thuringiensis* subsp. *israelensis*, or Bti for short, which is a biological control that is completely nontoxic to pets and people but kills fungus gnat larvae that eat it. To use it, sprinkle the recommended amount (according to instructions on the label) on top of the soil. Each time you water, the product releases Bti into the soil.

- *NATURAL CONTROL* BTI, PEROXIDE AND WATER, NEEM OIL, YELLOW STICKY TRAPS

MEALYBUGS

Usually more problematic in warmer climates, mealybugs basically suck the sap out of your plants like vampires. They look like tiny cotton balls and attach themselves to new growth in plant crevices, hiding along leaf midribs or down in the leaf axils where the leaves attach to the stem. The wooly mealybugs we see on our plants are usually females; the males are tiny winged insects that don't generally infest plants. To control them, dip a Q-tip in rubbing alcohol and dab it directly on the little bugs.

- *NATURAL CONTROL* NEEM OIL
- *MILD CONTROL* Q-TIP SOAKED IN ALCOHOL, INSECTICIDAL SOAP

APHIDS

Another sap sucker that does an immense amount of damage to young leaves, aphids generally infest plants in large groups. You'll have the most trouble with aphids when your plant is actively growing, because they love fresh, new growth and will completely distort leaves as they feed on the juices. As they feed, they excrete honeydew that attracts ants. Some species of ants will even farm aphids, protecting them from predators and consuming the sweet honeydew.

- *NATURAL CONTROL* WATER SPRAY, NEEM OIL, GREEN LACEWING LARVAE OR LADYBUGS (WHICH EAT APHIDS)
- *MILD CONTROL* INSECTICIDAL SOAP

CATERPILLARS

These are my worst enemies. Having open shade houses may be good for the plants, but butterflies and moths can also waltz (cha-cha?) right in and lay eggs on my plants, which eventually hatch into tiny, voracious anthurium-eating caterpillars. I have seen a perfect new leaf in the morning that by afternoon looks like someone shot it with buckshot.

- *NATURAL CONTROL* LEAF INSPECTION AND REMOVAL, NEEM OIL
- *MILD CONTROL* INSECTICIDAL SOAP, THURICIDE (BACTERIUM)
- *CHEMICAL CONTROL* PERMETHRIN INSECTICIDE

SPIDER MITES

Suffice it to say that I am not a fan of spider mites. You'll see fine webbing on your plants long before you see the mites that created them. These guys like dry conditions. I generally don't have spider mite problems on my outdoor plants, but some plants I bought from an enclosed greenhouse nursery that weren't properly quarantined were full of spider mites.

- *NATURAL CONTROL* NEEM OIL, PREDATORY MITES
- *MILD CONTROL* INSECTICIDAL SOAP
- *CHEMICAL CONTROL* MITICIDES SUCH AS AVID OR TALSTAR (MITES TEND TO DEVELOP RESISTANCE TO MITICIDES, SO ROTATE CHEMICALS. AND READ THE LABEL, BECAUSE THIS IS SERIOUS STUFF THAT CAN CAUSE IRRITATION TO YOUR EYES, SKIN, AND RESPIRATORY TRACT; INGESTING IT CAN CAUSE SERIOUS HEALTH ISSUES.)

Dealing with Diseases and Other Issues

Diseases can spread in large collections easily. When plants are growing close together indoors without proper air movement, diseases can get a foothold often before you even realize that there is a problem.

ERWINIA BLIGHT

This terrible bacterial disease is characterized by large patches of rot on the leaves and an awful smell. It spreads easily and quickly and can even be spread in recycled nursery water. Be sure to sterilize tools after using them on plants suffering with Erwinia blight, and dispose of affected leaves properly (not in your compost pile) if you detect it on a plant. To prevent Erwinia blight, water plants in the daytime so that the plant has a chance to dry, paying particular attention to keeping the leaves from getting wet, especially in areas with little air circulation.

- *TREATMENT* DITHANE FUNGICIDE, LIQUID COPPER SPRAY

XANTHOMONAS

Damage from Xanthomonas is usually concentrated around the perimeters of the leaves. This bacteria enters and attacks leaves, showing as yellow or brown dead tissue on leaf edges.

- *TREATMENT* PINCH OFF AFFECTED LEAVES OR REMOVE WITH STERILIZED CLIPPERS, USE PHYTON 27 BACTERICIDE/FUNGICIDE

TAN-COLORED LEAF SPOTS

These tiny leaf specks are usually more noticeable on darker colored leaves. The first time I saw them I thought some sort of fungus was to blame, because they appeared mostly in the summer, and summer here is hot and wet. After some research, I learned that the spots were the result of old spider mite damage.

- *TREATMENT* SPRAY WITH AVID MITICIDE/INSECTICIDE, USE BENEFICIAL PREDATORY MITES FOR INSECT CONTROL

CHLOROTIC OR YELLOWED LEAVES

Yellowed plant leaves are often the result of a lack of nitrogen. I see this quite often with plants grown in the ground in South Florida, because our soil is very nearly beach sand and has the nutritional value of Styrofoam. Nitrogen deficiency is characterized by weak, light green or yellow leaves with darker green veining.

- *TREATMENT* HIGH NITROGEN GRANULAR FERTILIZER

SUNBURN

Dry, tan, or brown patches on the surface of the leaves can often result from even a brief exposure to too much bright sun.

- *TREATMENT* REMOVE AFFECTED LEAVES AND MOVE THE PLANT TO A MORE SUITABLE LOWER-LIGHT SPACE

With all chemical controls, make sure you follow the directions on the label, exactly. Some of them may not be recommended for indoor use or around pets.

Digging Deeper

The plant world is always growing and changing so there's always more to learn and know, whether you enjoy plants as just a hobby or as an all-consuming passion. Many people enjoy plants so much they wonder if they can find a way to work with plants and make a living doing what they love. I think since Covid-19, more people than ever realize they want to feel fulfilled by their job, or at the very least, not dread going to work every day. There are so many ways to be surrounded by beautiful plants all day and still get paid. Whether you prefer to help other people learn about plants or you just want to work independently and have a quiet space to reflect, there is no better way to appreciate each day than working with plants. Here are a few ways you can learn about and get involved with growing plants.

Volunteering at Botanical Gardens

Botanical gardens often need volunteer help; you wouldn't believe how under-staffed most of them are. Through volunteers and donations, these special gardens are able to continue to provide for the care of all those beautiful plants that they share with their adoring public. If there's a local public garden in your area, make a call to find out who is in charge of volunteers, and offer your help. You'll learn so much from other plant people and by working with the plants—there are so many new skills to learn and cool people to meet when you volunteer.

Selling Plants

Your plants are going to grow, so you may as well propagate them and make a little extra income . . . so you can support your plant habit! It's never been easier to sell plants as a side hustle. If you sell online, you don't need your own website, because you can sell plants via any of the Facebook plant groups, on eBay, or on Etsy. You can also set up a booth and sell at plant shows or farmers' markets, or set up a pop-up nursery shop. With little overhead, you can rent out a space for the weekend and sell plants—and maybe even join other vendors to help draw people in. It takes some advertising, but I know a few people who have built successful businesses with pop-ups.

Alternatively, consider contacting local plant shops and asking if you can sell plants on consignment. You get paid when the shop sells your plants—it's as simple as that. This can be a great situation for the shop because it involves no overhead for them. It's a good idea to have a written agreement in place to ensure that there are no misunderstandings—for example, you need to consider what would happen if a customer returns a plant.

Working at a Nursery

A nursery near you may be looking for workers. Most nurseries hire workers for entry level positions all the way up to plant experts. There are so many things you could do—maintaining plants, providing customer service, and merchandising are a few examples. What better way to learn about plants than working in a nursery?

Taking Workshops and Classes

Lots of botanical gardens and nurseries offer workshops and classes on topics ranging from propagation and repotting, to hybridizing. You can learn new methods of growing plants from botanists and other experts. Plus, it's a great way to meet other like-minded plant people. In fact, if you have the plant know-how, why not approach some gardens and nurseries and ask if you can teach a plant-related workshop for them? You could offer the workshop for free or for a fee, and it would attract more customers and visitors to the shop. Ideas for workshops include repotting, how to divide houseplants, how to collect and create new plants from seed, how to set up a terrarium, and how to cross-pollinate plants.

Interning with a Grower

If you're more into the growing side than the sales side, or you're a little more introverted, you may be able to find a grower who could use some help and who would teach you the tricks of the trade. My favorite part of working with plants is growing them, and I'd prefer not to have to deal with selling them at all. Of course, if I didn't sell them, what would I do with all of them? There is just something magical about propagating plants, and for me, this is where the real rewards are.

Growing plants involves a lot more hot and heavy lifting work than you might expect, but it's totally worth the effort. I regularly throw fifty-pound bags of horticultural charcoal and potting soil over my shoulder to carry to my potting area. As many of the old-time growers begin to have trouble maintaining their collections, you may be a welcome help if you're trustworthy and can come by and help clean up under the benches and do other tasks that are more difficult to accomplish with age. I remember being silently judgmental when I would visit some older growers when I started out, because of the untidiness of their growing spaces. Plants everywhere. I thought that my shade house would never look like that. But after cleaning up after the last hurricane, I can see that once a collection falls into disrepair, it's tough to get it under control again. I wish that I had helped a few more people with their collections, but I was so busy with mine at the time.

Learning More About Aroids

The International Aroid Society (IAS) is a nonprofit organization that supports education and research. Joining the society and accessing its newsletters and website (www.aroid.org) are great ways for you to learn more about these amazing plants. In addition to researchers and growers, hobbyists and plant-curious folks are welcome to join. The IAS Annual Show and Sale usually occurs the third weekend in September at the Fairchild Tropical Botanical Garden in Coral Gables, Florida (barring any hurricanes!). In addition to the plant show, the event features a banquet and speakers. As of this writing, IAS has local chapters in the US Mid-Atlantic and West Coast areas, in Europe, and in Australia.

Resources for Plants and Supplies

In addition to the IAS Annual Show and Sale (see page 199), nurseries are great resources for aroid collectors. Here are a few of the best of them.

Arium Botanicals

https://ariumbotanicals.com

Arium Botanicals has curated its space as an urban conservatory for people getting their first plant and for avid collectors. The Portland, Oregon, shop focuses on implementing unusual plants in nature-focused designs and educating people to help them create green spaces. They also offer online plant sales. Along with education, they support both local and national artists by offering ceramic wares and homewares. Arium believes that plants are for everyone! Follow them on social media via Instagram and Facebook, @ariumbotanicals.

Brian's Botanicals

www.briansbotanicals.net

Brian Williams and his staff are plant people who have turned their love for plants into an online store. Based in Louisville, Kentucky, Brian's Botanicals specializes in rare and unusual plants, especially aroids such as colocasias and philodendrons. Over the years, their collection has expanded to include hardy tropical plants, rare and unusual plants, and terrarium plants. Though their concentration is in the Araceae family, their interest continues to grow across the plant kingdom. Collectors and breeders of tropical plants, Brian and his staff are continuously seeking out new plants to add to their collection and offer to customers. Their plants come from botanists, breeders, foreign seed companies, botanical gardens, and in trades with friends. Because so many sources of these unusual cultivars and species are now gone, they believe it is important to preserve these plants. Follow them on social media via Instagram and Facebook, @briansbotanicals.

Gabriella Plants

www.gabriellaplants.com

Gabriella Plants is a third-generation, family-owned nursery located in Oviedo, Florida, that specializes in growing and shipping tropical houseplants. Their motto is "Always Growing More," and it's for good reason: their teams work hard every day to grow more and ship plants directly from their greenhouses. Follow them on social media via Instagram and Facebook, @gabriellaplantsonline.

Glass Box Tropicals

www.glassboxtropicals.com

Glass Box Tropicals is an online provider with one of the largest selections of terrarium-specific plants available. They also offer select, hard-to-find houseplants, terrariums, and supplies for frog breeding and terrarium construction. Their plants and supplies are sustainably sourced from around the world, providing a vast selection of plants for your personal rainforest. Their current collection includes more than four hundred different plant species and hybrids in more than seventy-five genera. Their catalog of flora is consistently expanding, and they are always finding new terrarium-suitable plants from numerous global sources. Follow them on social media via Instagram and Facebook, @glassboxtropicals.

Greenhouse Megastore

http://greenhousemegastore.com

Greenhouse Megastore is an online source that is perfect for the professional and hobby grower alike. The store offers anything and everything a greenhouse professional, home gardener, or weekend warrior might need, including outdoor structures and coverings, containers, growing supplies, and hardware. I get my pots and mister heads here. They have everything! Follow them on social media via Instagram and Facebook, @greenhousemegastore.

ILLExotics

www.illexotics.com

Based in Philadelphia, ILLExotics is a boutique shop and online vendor that focuses on providing unique and uncommon houseplants from around the world, along with captive bred reptiles and amphibians, to their customers. They grow and source uncommon tropical plants from aroids to orchids, and fauna ranging from chameleons to dart frogs and invertebrates. Their business philosophy centers on urban sustainability. They also offer education regarding how to green-up your space and properly keep reptiles and amphibians as pets. Follow them on social media via Instagram and Facebook, @illexotics.

NSE Tropicals

www.nsetropicals.com

This is my online shop! More than just a nursery, we are serious plant collectors. We know firsthand the passion that drives a person to the ends of the earth to find that must-have plant. We know the ecstasy of finally locating a sought-after plant after years of searching. We are dedicated to bringing the odd, unusual, rare, exotic, or seemingly unattainable tropical plant to our fellow collectors. You will find just about anything imaginable from our online-only shop. Follow us on social media via Instagram and Facebook, @nsetropicals.

Tennessee Tropicals

www.tennesseetropicals.com

Tennessee Tropicals is a retail nursery and online plant shop that offers an amazing selection of rare and unusual tropical plants. Owner Calvin Owen has been growing and raising tropical plants for more than twenty-five years in Tennessee and prides himself on the quality of his plants and excellent service. He loves sharing his passion for plants and ships them across the country. Follow them on social media via Instagram and Facebook, @tennesseetropicals.

The Victorian Atlanta

www.thevictorianatlanta.com

The Victorian Atlanta was founded by husband and wife duo, Cary Smith and Libby Hockenberry, in Atlanta, Georgia. This creative plant shop strives to provide education about plants, tips for care, and rare plants that are potted in their quality handmade soil blends. They aim to inspire others to learn about plants and find the confidence to build on their green collections. The Victorian offers both common and uncommon desert and tropical species, along with hand-mixed soil blends and a range of beautiful planters and plant accessories. They also offer education about plants, plant consultations, and repotting services. Follow them on social media via Instagram and Facebook, @thevictorianatlanta.

Glossary of Terms

Aerial roots aboveground roots; often, these are adventitious roots that emerge from parts of the plants other than the root axis.

Anthesis the time during which a plant's flower is open or receptive to pollination. In aroids, this occurs at different times for male and female flowers.

Apical the apex or tip of an plant stem; its growing tip.

Appressed a growth habit in which leaves lie flat and close to the stem.

Axil the region (angle) between the back side of the leaf blade/petiole and the upper side of the stem.

Axillary buds small growth nodes located in the axil region, from which grow inflorescences in genera such as *Philodendron* and *Monstera*.

Basal located at the base of a plant organ such as a stem or leaf; often used in the context of basil veins that originate from the base of a leaf blade or inflorescences that emerge from the base of a plant.

Berry the fleshy fruit produced from a flower. Seeds are usually embedded in the berry pulp.

Botanical name a taxonomic convention of naming organisms using two components—the genus name and the species epithet; also called binomial or Latin name.

Bullate puckered or blistered texture in a leaf blade.

Chlorotic yellowing of leaves following lack of chlorophyll, resulting from iron deficiency, damaged roots, or excess water.

Climber a plant that grows vertically up a host tree or shrub as it develops using various mechanisms such as adhesive aerial roots.

Clone a genetically identical descendant of a plant created via asexual reproduction such as propagation from a plant cutting (stems or leaves).

Cross *see* hybrid.

Cultivar a plant bred for a particular characteristic or combination of characteristics that remains distinct, uniform, and stable in these characteristics when propagated by appropriate means.

Cutting plant material obtained by cutting and separating a piece of the stem, with the intent of using it for propagation.

Division plant material obtained by separating a clump of plants at the roots or by separating a rhizome or bulbil (small bulb).

Endemic a plant that is native to a specific region or locality.

Epiphyte a plant that germinates and lives attached to a host plant. Unlike parasites, epiphytic plants use the host plant only for support, and all required nutrition and moisture are derived from the air, rainfall, and debris surrounding them. Air plants are examples of epiphytes.

F1 generation offspring created from crossing two parents usually selected for specific desirable characteristics.

F2 generation offspring created by self-pollinating plants from the F1 generation of a hybrid line.

Fertile capable of producing fruit.

Fertilization the process of sexual reproduction in plants that occurs when pollen comes in contact with the ovule.

Genus a taxonomic classification that ranks above species and below family. In botanical nomenclature, the Latin name of a plant comprises a genus name followed by a species name.

Habit in the context of plants, refers to the shape, height, appearance, and form of growth.

Habitat the specific conditions in an area in which a plant species grows in the wild, such as temperature range, humidity, elevation, annual rainfall, and soil nutrient levels.

Hand pollination a method of artificial fertilization that involves collecting pollen from the male reproductive parts of a parent plant and applying it to the receptive female reproductive parts of another plant.

Hybrid an offspring of two plants of different cultivars, varieties, species, or genera created through sexual reproduction—when pollen of one plant is applied to the pistil (female part) of another.

In situ in the natural or original location; a plant in its natural range.

Inflorescence a flower-bearing branch or system of branches with no regular foliage between the flowers.

Infructescence the inflorescence at fruiting stage—a mass of fruits are considered one composite structure.

Internode a section of the stem between adjacent nodes.

Lumen a measure of the total amount of visible light emitted by a light source.

Margin the boundary of a plant organ, usually used in the context of leaves.

Midrib the large, central vein that runs along the midline of a leaf blade.

Natural hybrid a hybrid of two species that share a range usually created by common pollinators.

Node a point on the stem where a leaf is (or was) attached.

Offset a daughter plant that is genetically identical to the mother plant that emerges from the base of the mother plant.

Peltate shield shaped.

Pendulous hanging loosely or freely, in inflorescences or leaf orientation.

Perfect flower a flower that contains both male and female parts; also called a bisexual flower.

Petiole the stalk of a leaf that attaches the base of the leaf blade to the stem.

Pollen a powdery substance produced by male flowers that carry male reproductive cells.

Pollination the process of transferring pollen grains from the stamen (male reproductive parts) to the pistils (female reproductive parts) of a flower.

Population a group of plants of the same species that share a common area in their natural range.

Propagation the process of growing new plants from various sources such as seeds or cuttings of stems, leaves, or other viable plant parts.

Rhizome a subterranean stem that traverses horizontally (usually), has short internodes, roots downward, and pushes foliage/shoots upward.

Root hairs hairs growing along roots that significantly increase the available surface area for the roots to perform their absorption functions.

Roots parts of a plant that are usually subterranean and perform the functions of anchoring the plant, absorbing water and nutrients from the substrate and passing it to stem, and storing food.

Runner *see* stolon.

Section the grouping of aroids based on specific attributes and similarities.

Self-pollination the process of pollen from the stamen (male part) reaching the pistil (female part) of the same flower or a different flower in the same plant.

Shingle, shingling a growth habit in which the plant grows flat against its climbing structure, with overlapping leaves that resemble shingles.

Sinus the space between the two top lobes of a leaf.

Skototropic light-avoiding.

Spadix an inflorescence spike, usually in an aroid, with a thick axis that is lined with male and female flowers; it is surrounded by a spathe.

Spathe a modified leaf (bract) attached to the base of the spadix that usually forms a hood around the spadix to protect it.

Species the lowest principal rank in taxonomic hierarchy. Species names are usually written using a combination of genus name and a species epithet (in binomial nomenclature).

Sport a genetic mutation observed in a particular organ of a plant such as a branch, leaf, or stem that differs from the rest of the plant. It may be isolated and propagated to create a population of plants that share this mutation and thus qualify as cultivars.

Squamule a minute scale (hairlike structure) that appears flattened against the stem in aroids, especially in philodendron; for example, fuzzy squamules appear on *Philodendron serpens* and *P. verrucosum*. Its function is unknown.

Stigmatic fluid secretions by the stigma during the female receptive stage to improve the adhesion of pollen.

Stolon a creeping horizontal plant stem that emerges near the base of a stem that is specialized for vegetative reproduction, usually forming small leaves and roots at growth nodes.

Thermogenesis the metabolic process by which the spadix heats up when receptive to pollination.

Tissue culture a micropropagation technique used to propagate plants in large quantities by creating clones from very little vegetative material in a lab in a sterile nutrient solution such as agar.

Variegated exhibiting various colors in a plant organ such as leaves or stems.

About the Author

Enid Offolter is owner and founder of NSE Tropicals plant nursery. She loves to find unique and unusual plants, and is even in the process of getting a plant named after her (*Anthurium offolteranum* ined.). Her nursery boasts one of the largest personal collections of aroids in the United States. A two-time president of the International Aroid Society, she has given countless presentations to plant societies and garden clubs and has been profiled in the *New York Times* and appeared on Bloom & Grow Radio podcast, VICE TV, and the Plant One on Me YouTube channel.

Photo credit: Ivan Portilla

Acknowledgments

Turning an idea into a book is harder than it sounds. The following people made it all possible. I want to thank:

My NSE-orphaned son, Jesse, for feeding himself and generally staying alive on his own while I was working on this book. As of this writing, he is still going strong on peanut butter and jelly sandwiches.

The best photography team I could ever imagine, Sonya Revell and Elizabeth Jamie. Your insight and creativity know no bounds.

The team at Ten Speed Press, including designer Isabelle Gioffredi, art director Betsy Stromberg, production manager Serena Sigona, publicist Felix Cruz, marketer Andrea Portanova, and especially editor Lisa Regul—I couldn't have done it without you. Thank you for your patience and guiding me through this experience.

My agent, Michele Tessler, for getting this party started in the first place.

Siddharth, for always being right there with the answers when I needed quick help with fact checking and information. *Sid, what's this? Sid, what's that?*

Sam, Scott, and Mick who raced plants to me at the last minute when I needed them for the photos.

The massively supportive plant community for all their love and support.

And my sweet doggo, Athena, who passed away during the writing of this book.

Plant Photography Index

Index

Text copyright © 2022 by Enid Offolter
Photographs copyright © 2022 by Sonya Revell

All rights reserved.

Published in the United States by Ten Speed Press,
an imprint of Random House, a division of Penguin Random
House LLC, New York.
www.tenspeed.com

Ten Speed Press and the Ten Speed Press colophon are
registered trademarks of Penguin Random House LLC.

Library of Congress Cataloging-in-Publication Data
Names: Offolter, Enid, author.
Title: Welcome to the jungle : rare tropical houseplants to
      collect, grow, and love / Enid Offolter.
Other titles: Rare tropical houseplants to collect, grow,
      and love
Description: First edition. | Emeryville, California : Ten Speed
      Press, [2022] | Includes index and glossary.
Identifiers: LCCN 2021034250 (print) | LCCN 2021034251
      (ebook) | ISBN 9781984859945 (hardcover) | ISBN
      9781984859952 (ebook)
Subjects: LCSH: House plants. | Tropical plants. | Araceae. |
      Exotic plants.
Classification: LCC SB111 .O34 2021 (print) | LCC SB111
      (ebook) | DDC 635.9/65—dc23
LC record available at https://lccn.loc.gov/2021034250
LC ebook record available at https://lccn.loc.gov/2021034251

Hardcover ISBN: 978-1-9848-5994-5
eBook ISBN: 978-1-9848-5995-2

Printed in China

Editor: Lisa Regul
Designer: Isabelle Gioffredi | Art director: Betsy Stromberg
      | Production designers: Mari Gill and Faith Hague
Typefaces: Klim Type Foundry's Calibre by Kris Sowersby
      and Luzi Type's Messina by Luzi Gantenbein
Production manager: Serena Sigona
Prepress color manager: Nicholas Patton
Prop stylist: Elizabeth Jaime
Copyeditor: Lisa Theobald | Proofreader: Jean M. Blomquist
      | Indexer: Ken DellaPenta
Publicist: Felix Cruz | Marketer: Andrea Portanova

10 9 8 7 6 5 4 3 2 1

First Edition